What Causes Jesus To Work Miracles?

by
Norvel Hayes

Harrison House
Tulsa, Oklahoma

Unless otherwise indicated, all Scripture quotations are taken from the *King James Version* of the Bible.

What Causes Jesus To Work Miracles?
ISBN 0-89274-788-9

P.O. Box 1379
Cleveland, Tennessee 37311

Published by Harrison House, Inc.
P.O. Box 35035
Tulsa, Oklahoma 74153

Printed in the United States of America.

Contents

Introduction

Before we get into the message that God has placed on my heart, I would like to share with you something of my background so you can see how the Lord has dealt with me about the Church and His will for it.

Some time ago the Spirit of the Lord moved upon me and called me to start a Bible school and teach His Word. I haven't been a Bible teacher all my life, and I don't even know why God would call me to do that. I didn't understand it then, and I still don't understand it now, but He does.

As far as the world was concerned, I was an executive, even though I was a school dropout. I was born into a denominational family, and when I was just ten years old, my mother died with cancer. I couldn't understand why she died and left us three children all alone. Neither did anyone else we knew. We just assumed that it was the Lord's will. We said that God knew what He was doing.

I had a little sister about two years old, and a brother who was fourteen. When he was about seventeen and in high school playing football he became sick and later died at the age of nineteen. After your mother dies and your only brother dies, you just kind of give up on everything.

So I dropped out of school as soon as I could and went off to Knoxville, Tennessee, where I got a job. In time I became a pool hustler. Later I got a job traveling to colleges and universities. The first year or so I just broke even, but afterwards I began to make money. My father had taught me how to work. I remember as a teenager working hard for ten or twelve long, sweaty hours at a stretch for twenty-five cents a day. People didn't pay much in those days.

After a while on my new job I got to making a hundred dollars a day. About two or three years later, I was making a thousand dollars a day. When you start making four, five, six or seven thousand dollars a week, it doesn't take long to get rich. In the eyes of the world, since I had money I was happy. I was the same way. Like everybody else, I thought that money bought happiness. But it didn't, and I didn't know why not.

So I just kept working and making money, until one day I became a business executive. Then I went from being an executive to owning the whole manufacturing company I was working for.

"Now, I'll be happy," I thought.

But I wasn't.

Soon I bought myself a mansion, four Cadillacs and some tailor-made suits and was going to Broadway shows, playing golf at the country club and doing all the things that go with the life of success — but I was empty in my heart and confused in my head.

I was a sales manager and had taught myself how to sell. After I owned the place, I taught my supervisors how to sell. That was the extent of my teaching. I was tremendously successful, but my life was empty, and I didn't know why. I began to think about my future. I began to wonder if I died, if I would go to hell or not. I didn't know for sure.

Answering God's Call

One day while I was on a business trip to Georgia Tech, I just got tired of having money but no happiness and peace of mind. So I fell on my knees and gave my life to God. I didn't feel a thing when I did it, I just did it.

The next week I was driving in my Cadillac from a stockholders' meeting in Columbus, Ohio, back to Indianapolis, Indiana, where I lived at the time. As I drove along Highway 40 I began to say a little prayer. All of a sudden, it was as if a shock went through me. The Lord came right down into that car with me, and I broke down in tears.

Now I was a hard-nosed business executive who didn't cry for anybody or anything. I was tough. I handled my employees with authority, telling them exactly what to do, and if they didn't do it, I fired them. I tried to be kind as a person, but I was strong and strict as a businessman. That's the reason I was so successful.

I was basically an honest man. I wouldn't cheat anybody out of anything, but my life really didn't belong to God; it belonged to me. I worked hard and didn't expect something for nothing. I went out and made what I wanted. But I was empty, and so the Lord came into my car and told me that He wanted me to come and follow Him.

I couldn't believe that it was happening to me, but it did happen. I cried for an hour and a half, all the way from Columbus, Ohio, to the city limits of Richmond, Indiana.

When I got home, I thought everyone in my family would be pleased that the Lord Jesus had come and visited me in my car. I walked into the house, and they asked me, "What happened to you? You look like a ghost."

"There's no use in telling you what happened to me," I said, "because you wouldn't believe it. I don't even know if I believe it myself or not. But it happened anyway."

Then I went on to tell them how Jesus had come to me and had talked to me for an hour and a half. I told them that He said He wanted me.

"Oh, I don't know about that," they said.

"Yes, I've given my life to Him," I told them. "I'm going to do whatever He wants me to do."

At that time I didn't know anything about God except what little I had heard in church. Just because you go to church doesn't mean that you know the Lord, and I didn't. I had given my life to Him, but I had never given my heart to Him. I knew nothing about Him. So I went to my pastor because I thought he knew the Lord much better than I did.

At this time in my life, I knew nothing about Pentecostalism. I didn't even know there were people on earth who talked in tongues, laid hands on people and prayed for healing. But later on, I came into contact with a Pentecostal Full-Gospel preacher. When I went to talk to him about my visit from the Lord, I asked him, "What do you think will happen to me?"

"Well, I don't know," he told me.

"The call of God is so strong on me I can hardly stand it," I said, "and I don't even know anything about God. What does He want *me* for? What does He want me to do?"

To tell the truth, I really didn't want to get involved in ministry because I could see that my family was not going to accept it. But I told the Lord, "God, I'm available, but You're going to have to train me. I'll do whatever You say for me to do."

So He sent me to the city dump!

For what? To work for Him.

What did I do at the city dump? I witnessed to people about Jesus. They were so goofed up, they would listen to anybody. Then I would take some money out of my pocket and give it to them. I fed them and prayed for them from shack to filthy, stinking shack, because that's how they lived — in poverty, total poverty.

God Is a God of Faith

I went on ministering in the city dump and elsewhere for months on end. Then one day while I was working in the dump, the Lord spoke to me and said, "If you'll be faithful to Me here, I'll promote you."

Every time I stand up to minister to a crowd of thousands now, I think about that time and remember what God told me that day in the city dump.

After seven long years, the Lord spoke to me again and said, "I want you to start studying the Bible on the subject of faith."

"Oh, yeah, faith," I said. "What's that?"

That's how ignorant I was of spiritual things. So I started studying the Bible, and I discovered that if anybody on earth can believe for something before he sees it, then he will get it.

Do you understand that? If you can believe God for something *before* you see it, then you will get it! If you're waiting to see it to believe it, then you're not going to receive it, because that's not the way faith works.

God is a faith-God. The only way He operates is through faith.

Faith in what? Faith in Jesus as our Savior first then faith in Him to meet our needs on earth.

In the Bible, the Lord has promised us everything we need. If we have faith for it, if we can believe before we see it, then He will give it to us. It's just that simple.

It's too bad that most people in the Church have not discovered that yet.

You can hear Kenneth Hagin or Lester Sumrall or someone else preach faith, but it won't do you a bit of good if it's only head knowledge to you. It won't work for you the way it works for them if all you have is head knowledge, not heart knowledge. If you want faith to work for you, you have to get it on the inside of you, down in your spirit.

The Word of God only works for those who get it on the inside of them, those who put first things first in their daily lives. That means putting the Lord first. If you never learn to put first things first, you will always be second, third, fourth, fifth, sixth, seventh or eighth. What does that mean? It means that you will be somewhere out in God's permissive will, but not in His perfect will.

God's Permissive Will and His Perfect Will

Many years ago the Lord appeared to Kenneth Hagin in the hospital and talked to him for an hour and a half. One of the things He told him was, "The reason many people die young and don't live out their full lives is because they are operating in My permissive will. They never strive to get into My perfect will — and it costs them their lives."

That night God told Brother Hagin, "It's a good thing you're lying in this hospital and can't get up so I can come and talk to you, because if I don't, you are going to die in seven years."

At the time Brother Hagin was only forty-eight years old.

"You are going to die in seven years," the Lord said to him, "because you have been refusing to prophesy when My Spirit has come upon you, and it's going to cost you your life."

Does that mean that God would let someone like Kenneth Hagin die just because he refused to prophesy? You'd better believe it!

When you have been called to do something and don't do it, in the eyes of the Lord that is **rebellion** which **is as the sin of witchcraft** (1 Sam. 15:23).

So, my brother or sister, I don't have any choice but to share with you the message recorded in this book. The Lord has shown me that the reason the Church is in trouble today, as far as getting His power to manifest itself, is because it is sadly lacking in the four areas we are about to discuss: worship, faith, work, and knowledge and obedience.

1
Miracles Come Through *Worship* — Worshipping in Spirit and in Truth

1

Miracles Come Through *Worship* — Worshipping in Spirit and in Truth

Take my yoke upon you, and learn of me; for I am meek and lowly in heart: and ye shall find rest unto your souls.

Matthew 11:29

When God called me to serve Him by teaching others about Him and His Word, I didn't know anything about Him. I had to learn everything about God. The only thing I knew was that He saved people.

The church I had been raised in taught about salvation, but it did not hold healing services. There were no miracles or gifts of the Spirit in evidence in it. It was orderly and restrained. Each week it printed up bulletins that told the hours of Sunday school and church services, but the congregation never really worshipped. We were taught to come in, sit quietly, and be nice.

We needed to do what Jesus says in Matthew 11:29: learn of Him.

"Learn what?"

Learn responsibility to God.

"Take My Yoke Upon You... and...Find Rest Unto Your Souls"

Jesus tells us to take His yoke upon us and learn of Him because He is meek and lowly in heart and in Him we will find rest to our souls.

I want you to know that I am a man who has found rest in my soul. I haven't had a bad day in years. I haven't had an unsuccessful day in years. I haven't had a confused day in years.

I don't have sad days because God doesn't have sad days. I don't believe in having sad days. I believe that in Christ all of our days are supposed to be full of life, full of joy, full of passion, full of victory. Not just some of them — every one of them.

Our days on this earth are precious. There is coming a time when they will all be gone. The Bible says that our life is like the grass, one day it is here, and the next it is withered and dead. (James 1:10,11.)

One of these days your life will be over, and people will hardly notice that you are gone. If you want to do anything for God, you had better do it now. So one of the first steps in getting Jesus to work miracles in your life is to take His yoke upon you and learn of Him.

Learn about Jesus. Learn Who He is, and how He fulfills your life in every way. If you will do that, then you won't have any sad days either.

"For My Yoke Is Easy, and My Burden Is Light"

For my yoke is easy, and my burden is light.
Matthew 11:30

What does Jesus mean when He says that His yoke is easy?

We know that the yoke of sickness is not easy, it's hard. More than that, it's deadly. The yoke of cancer will kill you, just as it killed my mother. The yoke of kidney disease will kill you, just as it killed my brother.

Yet Jesus tells us that His yoke is easy. That means that if you and I will give up totally, life will be so easy for us. Receiving miracles from God is not hard, as most people think. It's easy.

"Are you kidding?"

No, not at all. In Romans 10:17 we are told that faith comes by hearing, and hearing by the Word of God. So if you can hear and believe, then you can receive miracles from God. But in order to hear, you must first listen to the Lord Jesus Christ. If you are not going to listen to Jesus, then you are going to be in trouble the rest of your life, bad trouble. All your worship is going to be in vain.

Worshipping in Vain

> **This people draweth nigh unto me with their mouth, and honoureth me with their lips; but their heart is far from me.**
>
> **But in vain they do worship me, teaching for doctrines the commandments of men.**
>
> **Matthew 15:8,9**

What does Jesus mean when He talks about drawing near to God with our mouths and honoring Him with our lips but worshipping Him in vain? He is talking about announcing church services at eleven o'clock on Sunday morning, but never really worshipping God.

When Jesus says that we worship in vain, He means that our worship doesn't count. If we are going to truly worship the Lord, then we are going to have to worship Him in spirit and in truth. (John 4:24.) And that means putting Him first in our lives.

"You Shall Have No Other Gods Before Me"

...Thou shalt love the Lord thy God with all thy heart, and with all thy soul, and with all thy strength, and with all thy mind; and thy neighbour as thyself.

Luke 10:27

One time a lawyer came to Jesus and asked Him, "What do I have to do to have eternal life?"

Jesus said to him, "You're an expert in the law. How do you read it?"

The man said, "You shall love the Lord your God with all your heart, and all your soul, and all your strength, and all your mind, and you shall love your neighbor as yourself."

"That's right," said Jesus. "Do these things, and you will live." (Luke 10:25-28, author's paraphrase.)

To love the Lord our God with all our heart and soul and strength and mind means to put Him first before all other things. In the Ten Commandments the Lord says that we are to have no other gods before Him. (Ex. 20:3.)

If you will do that, if you will put God first in your life, if you will spend time truly worshipping Him in spirit and in truth, then He will put you first and will perform miracles on your behalf.

To See Miracles, Bring Forth Fruit

Ye have not chosen me, but I have chosen you, and ordained you, that ye should go and bring forth fruit, and that your fruit should remain: that whatsoever ye shall ask of the Father in my name, he may give it you.

John 15:16

Do you remember when John the Baptist was preaching repentance and baptizing people in the River Jordan? Some of the Pharisees and Sadducees came to him and asked to be baptized. He said to them, "Where's your fruit? I'm not going to baptize you until you bring fruit to the Lord!"

"What fruit?" they asked.

And John went on to remind them that every tree that does not bring forth good fruit will be cut down and cast into the fire. (Matt. 3:7-10, author's paraphrase.)

When the Bible talks about trees here, it is talking about people, about you and me. If you are sitting there in your easy chair praying, "Oh, Lord, I need You to perform a miracle for me," but you are producing no fruit for the Kingdom of God, then you are worshipping in vain. You had better get started winning some souls and bringing some tithes into the storehouse, because your life will soon be over and you only get one chance to do what the Lord has told you to do — bear much fruit.

John the Baptist told the Pharisees and Sadducees, "Don't give me this thing about being the sons of Abraham. The God I serve can raise up sons of Abraham from these stones if He so chooses. So don't tell me that Abraham is your relative. I won't buy that. If Abraham is your relative, then you will prove it by bringing fruit to God." (Matt. 3:9, author's paraphrase.)

So the people asked John, "Well then, what should we do?"

His answer was, "If you have two coats, give one of them to someone who has none. If you have meat to eat and someone else doesn't, share your meat with him." (Luke 3:11, author's paraphrase.)

Most churches don't preach that kind of Gospel anymore. But that's what John the Baptist preached, and Jesus said that there was no greater prophet born of woman than John the Baptist. (Luke 7:28.)

If you want to see the Lord work miracles for you, then bring forth fruit.

Keep on Praying and Worshipping

If you will take the advice that Jesus gave the lawyer, your problem days will be over, and your miracle days will begin. I'm not talking just about healing miracles. I'm talking about all kinds of miracles: financial miracles, marriage miracles, business miracles, miracles for your children.

I know what it's like to have a devil-possessed, drug-addicted child that no one can reach or help. My daughter was so bad off that I had the best ministers in the land come to my house and try to reach her. They would talk to her and she would seem to listen, but she kept right on taking dope — so I just kept right on praying and worshipping the Lord.

The reason I kept right on praying and worshipping the Lord is that I knew that five of her friends had died. They were all part of a group of about ten youngsters who ran around together. They would go to nightclubs and horse races and beach parties. Five of them ended up dead, and I didn't want that to happen to my daughter.

I would pray that God would send down His angels and protect her. I knew that she and her friends would do things like get out on the highway on weekends and see how fast they could take the curves without turning over. Or they would try to outrun the police with all ten of them in one car and high on drugs. They would do all sorts of goofed-up, devilish things. As a result, some of them ended up overdosing on drugs, drowning in the lake or catching themselves on fire. But through it all, I just kept on praying — even though I was seeing no results in the natural.

So I know what you are going through in your home. I know the hell of living in a house with a devil-possessed child. I know what it's like to love that child with all of your being. I know what it's like to remember the good times you had together when that child was growing up, going swimming and on picnics together. I know what it's like to recall that child climbing up into your lap at bedtime. I know what it's like to relive all those precious, innocent times.

I also know what it's like to go to five funerals and stand looking down at the lifeless bodies of five young people lying dead in caskets. I tell you, that kind of thing will make a believer out of you that the devil is real and that he is out to kill, steal and destroy you and your family. (John 10:10.)

Every time I went to a funeral for one of those youngsters, Satan would tell me, "Your child is next. Yours will be next. Yours will be next." But I just kept on trusting God. I kept right on praying and confessing, binding the devil and worshipping the Lord.

Do you ever get discouraged? I don't. I don't get discouraged about anything. I absolutely refuse to get discouraged. All the time this misery was going on, I would go off every weekend to Dallas or Albuquerque or New York or some place else to hold meetings and win other men's children to God. The devil would accuse me, through other people who would come to me and ask, "Doesn't it make you feel funny to win other people's kids when you can't save your own?"

I tell you, it made me want to knock them in the head, because they didn't have any sense. Such people have no appreciation for the Gospel. That's why the next moment I would repent and feel sorry for them.

So I would say to them, "Yes, I'm going to Dallas next weekend, and Albuquerque the next weekend, and New York the next weekend. The next time you see me, I'll be winning souls to Jesus, laying hands on the sick, casting out devils and helping people to receive miracles."

So I know exactly how the woman felt who came to Jesus to ask Him for a miracle for her daughter who was possessed with a demon.

The Woman With the Demon-Possessed Daughter

Then Jesus went thence, and departed into the coasts of Tyre and Sidon.

And, behold, a woman of Canaan came out of the same coasts, and cried unto him, saying, Have mercy on me, O Lord, thou Son of David; my daughter is grievously vexed with a devil.

But he answered her not a word. And his disciples came and besought him, saying, Send her away; for she crieth after us.

But he answered and said, I am not sent but unto the lost sheep of the house of Israel.

Matthew 15:21-24

This woman came to Jesus crying out to Him, "Lord, help me. I have a child, a daughter, who is possessed of the devil."

I know exactly how she felt. I know what it's like to be in a situation in which you can't help your child, you can't reach her, all you can do is try to find some way to keep her out of the clutches of the devil.

So this woman came to Jesus in desperation, crying out to Him for mercy. But the Lord wouldn't even speak to her.

You see, just because we pray, even out of extreme need, doesn't mean that the Lord will hear or respond to our prayer. There wasn't anything wrong with this woman's prayer except that she was praying selfishly.

I know what that is like too. I did the same thing for a long time. I tried with all my might to pray down God's mercy on my daughter. It took me three years to learn what I was doing wrong. This woman was smarter than I was. It only took her a few minutes to learn.

God doesn't respond to ignorance. He says, **My people are destroyed for lack of knowledge** (Hos. 4:6). If you are ignorant, God can't bless you. My brother or sister, God is not ignorant, and He doesn't deal in ignorance — not in any shape, form or fashion. He deals in truth, and in faith in Him and His eternal Word.

When You Pray, Believe You Receive

> **Therefore I say unto you, What things soever ye desire, when ye pray, believe that ye receive them, and ye shall have them.**
>
> **Mark 11:24**

The Lord did not answer this woman a single word. Why? Because He is not interested in seeing things our way. I know, because I spent years praying for my devil-possessed daughter, and nothing happened. It was just as though God didn't even hear me.

You and I are living under the dispensation of faith. That means that when we pray for something, we have to believe that we have it before we can see it manifested. That's why once we ask for something in prayer, we must not give up.

Faith never gives up. Faith never sees the pitfalls from the prayer to the manifestation. Real faith, the Abraham-founded faith, goes on day after day, month after month, year after year if necessary, saying, "It's mine. In Jesus' name, it's mine."

That's what I learned to do. I learned to stand firm in faith against the devil, saying to him, "Devil, you will not destroy my daughter. I know you have done that to some of her friends, but you will not do it to her. In the name of Jesus I declare that you cannot have her."

Worship the Lord!

Then came she and worshipped him, saying, Lord, help me.

But he answered and said, It is not meet to take the children's bread, and to cast it to dogs.

And she said, Truth, Lord: yet the dogs eat of the crumbs which fall from their masters' table.

Then Jesus answered and said unto her, O woman, great is thy faith: be it unto thee even as thou wilt. And her daughter was made whole from that very hour.

Matthew 15:25-28

Like this woman, I just kept on worshipping God. I kept on passing out tracts, kept on doing the things that I knew the Lord had called me to do. If you will do that, if you will keep on doing what God has called you to do, you will discover that God will do for you what He has promised in His Word.

No human could help my daughter. She was too far gone for that. Do you know how she was finally set free of demon-possession? The Lord sent an angel into her room and it scared her out of her wits. Do you know why she was so scared? Because that angel who came into her room and sat down on the side of her bed was as big as two men. When you are that big and you come from heaven, all you have to do is show up. My daughter was so scared she couldn't say a word.

Then the angel got up and started walking down the hallway. My daughter jumped up out of bed and followed after him. She saw him go down the hall, turn left and disappear right through the wall! She was really scared then, so scared that her whole life was changed forever.

But that was all right with me. I didn't care how the Lord did it, as long as He did it. Blessed be the name of the Lord!

You might say, "But, Brother Norvel, isn't there some other way to get the Lord to manifest Himself and perform miracles? Surely there must be an easier way to find favor with God than praying for three years."

Yes, there is. I am sorry to say that the reason it took so long for me in that situation is because I was so ignorant about the things of God. If I had known then what I know now, it could have been done much quicker. I would have spent less time praying to the Lord and more time worshipping Him.

You see, the more time you spend worshipping the Lord, the more favor you find with Him. If you want the Lord to do great things for you, then you need to spend a great deal of time in worship to Him.

What did the woman do to get the Lord's attention? What can you and I do to get Him to work miracles for us? The answer is found in verse 25: **Then came she and *worshipped him*....**

Put to the Test

Now it is true that once the woman began to worship Him, the Lord put her through a little test before He answered her prayer. He told her that it was not right for Him to take the (Hebrew) children's bread and give it to (Gentile) dogs.

Her answer was, in essence, "Lord, I don't care what You call me, You are my Lord and Master. I will go on worshipping You the rest of my life."

When she said that, He told her that she had great faith and that her request was granted, that her daughter was made completely whole "from that very hour."

Now notice that the woman wasn't even present with her daughter when she was made whole. Where was she? She was off worshipping the Lord!

That's where you and I ought to be in our times of trial and tribulation. If we will stand the test, if we will remain faithful to the Lord, if we will go right on worshipping and serving Him in spite of our circumstances, in time we too will receive the answer to our prayers.

Learn To Put First Things First

> **But seek ye first the kingdom of God, and his righteousness; and all these things shall be added unto you.**
>
> **Matthew 6:33**

Jesus has told us to take His yoke upon us and learn of Him.

Don't be religiously brainwashed to the point that you just drive yourself up the wall. Don't become so busy doing all the right things that you forget to spend time worshipping the Lord. Don't become so involved in schedules and programs that you neglect worship. Yes, work hard for the Lord. But just be sure that you give as much time to worship as you do to work.

Remember, Jesus said that His yoke is easy, and His burden is light.

It's a matter of priority. Learn to put first things first in your life.

"Well, what will happen if I do that?"

You will get total victory in life.

"You mean that if I put God first, He will work miracles for me?"

All the time.

He will work miracles in your body. He will make you strong and healthy.

He will work miracles in your mind. He will make it keener and sharper than ever before.

He will work miracles in your spirit. The gifts of the Holy Spirit will begin to flow through you. The Spirit of the Lord will manifest Himself through you as He wills. (1 Cor. 12:11.)

Whenever you need something from the Lord, the Holy Spirit will rise up within you and give you the particular gift you need most to help you win the victory in that situation.

If you are ignorant of the gifts of the Spirit, then you need to read the twelfth chapter of 1 Corinthians. The gifts of the Spirit won't work for you unless you know about them.

Remember, the only part of God's Word that works for you is that part you know for yourself. If you never study the Bible, God will never be able to do much for you. You may go to church and receive a blessing in the service, but you won't really get in on the great miracles of God — only the overflow.

If you want the Lord to perform real miracles in your life, then you are going to have to *know* what He says, boldly *proclaim* what He says and then *do* what He says. If you will do that, then the Lord will come to you, give you favor with Him and with others, and perform any miracle you may need.

"Any miracle I need?"

Absolutely any kind. It doesn't matter what it is.

Put Your Faith Into Action!

Even so faith, if it hath not works, is dead, being alone.

James 2:17

Remember, the woman's demon-possessed daughter was delivered and set free "that very hour" because the woman put first things first and worshipped the Lord.

"Will He do that same thing for me?"

He will if you can believe it.

Now I'm not talking about believing with your head, I'm talking about believing with your heart — and your hands and feet — putting your faith in action!

It won't do you a bit of good to believe something with your head, or even to speak it forth from your mouth, if you are not going to act on what you say you believe.

James tells us that without action, faith is dead. God wants to see us on our knees worshipping Him, on our faces worshipping Him, and on our feet worshipping Him. He wants to see us praising Him in private as well as in public.

The Bible says that when you do alms, do them in secret, and God will reward you openly. (Matt. 6:3,4.) What you do in secret, God will reward openly. Get alone before God and worship and praise Him.

No wonder so many pastors have such great success in their ministries. It's because they spend time praying, praising and worshipping the Lord, asking Him to anoint their services and to work miracles, signs and wonders just as the first apostles did in the book of Acts. (Acts 4:24-30.)

If you and I would do that, if we would spend twenty or thirty minutes in earnest prayer, praise and worship before we go into church, we would see healing services like we have never experienced before in our lives.

That's the way it is supposed to be. If we could ever do as the first apostles did and get ourselves into "one accord" (Acts 2:1) — in prayer, praise and worship to the Lord — we would see God work mighty miracles in our midst.

Praise and Worship

...Thou shalt worship the Lord thy God, and him only shalt thou serve.

Luke 4:8

There is a vast difference between praising the Lord and worshipping Him. It is possible to praise the Lord continually — morning, noon and night — and that is good. That is what we are supposed to do. In His day, Jesus said that if the people did not praise Him, the very stones would cry out. (Luke 19:37-40.)

God loves praise. But in order to worship, you must get beyond praise. You must shut yourself off from the world and begin to cry out to Him from the depths of your being:

"Oh, God, there is none like You on the earth, none. You are altogether holy and righteous. I come into Your presence asking that You give me in my life and ministry only that which I truly need. Never let me seek a blessing that I cannot handle, one that would destroy me.

"Lord, help me never to put anyone or anything ahead of You and Your Kingdom.

"Father, I worship You. I want to be close to You. There are no other gods in my life, You only do I worship and serve."

When you go to worship the Lord, remove your family from your focus. Remove your pocketbook from your thoughts. Remove your ministry from your mind. For that period of time — whether it's thirty minutes or forty-five minutes a day — remove everything from your heart and soul that would keep you from devoting full attention to the Lord. Worship Him only. That is what He demands and deserves. Nothing else will do.

It is good to worship with your family and with your church, but worship God in secret. What God sees you do in secret, He will reward openly. How will He do it? He will do it by seeing that you never have a sad day, never have a financial need that can't be met, never face a problem that can't be solved, never encounter a challenge that won't end in total victory.

If you will enter into God's holy presence, you will always have peace. You will always have patience. You will always have plenty.

You will be amazed at the miracles that the Lord will perform for you. He will send His angels to watch over you and protect you and guide you and work on your behalf. (Ps. 91.)

If you have a need in your life right now that is about to drive you up the wall, the greatest thing that you can possibly do is to spend time worshipping the Lord.

Worship Leads to Healing

When he was come down from the mountain, great multitudes followed him.

And, behold, there came a leper and worshipped him, saying, Lord, if thou wilt, thou canst make me clean.

And Jesus put forth his hand, and touched him, saying, I will; be thou clean. And immediately his leprosy was cleansed.

Matthew 8:1-3

What did the leper do when he came to Jesus for healing?

He *worshipped* Him.

Then when he asked Jesus to heal him, the Lord reached out His hand and touched him, and *immediately* His leprosy was cleansed.

How did this man get his healing from the Lord? Did he go to a healing service? Did he hunt down fourteen healing evangelists and have them lay hands on him and pray?

No, he worshipped the Lord, and the miracle happened to him. He found favor with the Lord, and when he experienced the touch of the Master's hand, the skin of his entire body was made like new and he was made whole.

I have seen many such miracles in my ministry. One time I was ministering in an Assembly of God church in Mississippi when a man came to me with skin cancer all over his body. He said to me, "I want Jesus to remove this."

I reached out and touched him in Jesus' name. I cursed that cancer and commanded it to die and to remove itself from him. He turned around to sit down. It had only been about four or five seconds since I had touched him. As he went to take his seat in the pew, he suddenly cried out, "My hands are new! Look, I've got new skin on me. Look at me, look at me, look at me!"

The Lord has not changed. What Jesus did in His days of ministry on the earth, He will do in our day.

Just as He delivered this woman's demon-possessed child, He will deliver our children from the devil.

Just as He healed this man of skin cancer, He will heal us of our diseases.

Worship Brings Peace of Mind and Heart

> **Be careful for nothing; but in every thing by prayer and supplication with thanksgiving let your requests be made known unto God.**
>
> **And the peace of God, which passeth all understanding, shall keep your hearts and minds through Christ Jesus.**
>
> **Philippians 4:6,7**

But we must remember that in order to receive a miracle from the Lord, we must put first things first. We must worship the Lord. We must cut ourselves off from everyone and everything else and enter into worship, focusing our attention totally upon Him.

As you do that, think about the goodness of the Lord. Think about His death on the cross. Think about His blood that was shed so that you and your family might be set free. Think about His limitless love and grace and power.

Get your mind off yourself and your need and onto the Lord and His righteousness and His Kingdom. Give praise and glory to God. Worship Him in spirit and in truth.

Spend time every day worshipping God. Stand firm against the devil who will try to steal and kill and destroy you and your family. If you will do these things, the Lord will give you revelation knowledge about what the devil is planning so that you can pray and defeat him and his works.

Surrender your life and your heart to the Lord. Worship Him and give Him thanks continually. Confess His Word over yourself and your loved ones, and the peace that passes all understanding will keep your heart and mind in the love of God Who will perform mighty miracles on your behalf.

To Him be the glory forever and ever!

2

Miracles Come Through *Faith* — God Will Perform His Word

2

Miracles Come Through *Faith* — God Will Perform His Word

...If thou canst believe, all things are possible to him that believeth.

Mark 9:23

God performs all kinds of miracles. He is a miracle-working God — always has been and always will be. He will work miracles right now for anybody, including you. But He will do for you only what you believe Him to do.

Whatever I have believed God for, He has given me. If I believe Him long enough, and if my faith does not waver, I always get what I ask in prayer. Never in my Christian experience have I ever asked and believed God for anything that I did not receive from Him in due time — that is, anything that is promised me in the Bible.

You must understand that when you pray and believe, your prayer and belief must be scriptural. You can't just say, "Oh, I think I'll believe God for $10 million by next Friday." You can forget that. I'm not talking about asking or believing for just whatever comes into your head. I'm talking about asking and believing and receiving what God has clearly promised in His Word.

God will give you what He has promised you — and the best part is that it's all free. It's yours for the asking, or I should say, it's yours for the believing, which is the second thing you must do to get the Lord to work miracles for you. Besides worshipping God, you must also have faith in Him and in His Word.

Seek the Lord and Prosper

> **Then all the people of Judah took Uzziah, who was sixteen years old, and made him king in the room of his father Amaziah....**
>
> **And he sought God in the days of Zechariah, who had understanding in the visions of God: and as long as he sought the Lord, God made him to prosper.**
>
> **2 Chronicles 26:1,5**

Several years ago, my daughter developed strange growths all over her body. For three years I prayed and prayed, but the growths were still there. All during this time, I kept seeking the Lord for truth. I discovered this passage in 2 Chronicles that says that as long as King Uzziah sought God, the Lord made him to prosper.

As long as you seek God, you will prosper too. If there is something you don't know, then ask the Lord and He will reveal the truth to you. (James 1:5.) That's what He did for me in this situation.

I began to seek the Lord because I had been praying so long without any results. How would you feel if you had a child with forty-seven horrible growths on her body, and you had been asking God to remove them for three long years with no sign of an answer?

These growths were terrible. They would break open and bleed. My daughter had the ugliest hands of anybody in her high school. I knew it would take a miracle from God to get those growths to go away, but I didn't know how to get that miracle. I kept praying and praying, but nothing happened. So finally I began to seek God for knowledge and understanding.

I know now that I could have prayed for ten more years, and it would not have done a bit of good. She could have wound up with even more growths than ever.

So when I finally realized that my prayers were not working and were not going to work, I turned to the Lord for answers. I told Him that I really wanted to know the truth.

After I had sought the Lord for some time, one night I was walking through my living room after church on Sunday evening. I didn't have any idea that anything unusual was going to happen to me that night. I don't consider myself a special person any more than any other Christian. I wasn't expecting anything out of the ordinary to take place. In fact, I didn't even know that God did things like He was about to do for me, but of course the Bible says He does.

In 2 Corinthians 12:2 the apostle Paul tells how he was caught up "to the third heaven." In verses 3 and 4 he goes on to say that all of a sudden he found himself in paradise.

That same thing happened to me.

"Believe and Not Doubt!"

For verily I say unto you, That whosoever shall say unto this mountain, Be thou removed, and be thou cast into the sea; and shall not doubt in his heart, but shall believe that those things which he saith shall come to pass; he shall have whatsoever he saith.

Mark 11:23

As I was walking across the living room, suddenly I took a step, and I began to leave my body and rise into another world, where God is. Since then, I have had the privilege of being taken up into heaven to be shown some things, but this time I didn't see anything. All I knew was that I was slipping out of my body and going into another world.

When I got far enough into that other world, the Lord began to talk to me. He asked me, "How long are you going to put up with those growths on your daughter's body?"

Now He said this boldly. It wasn't one of those sweet messages like, "I love you, son. Your prayers have been heard. Just stay faithful to Me and keep on praying, and one of these days I'll remove those growths from your daughter's body."

No, He wasn't saying that one of these days He was going to make my child well, just as He is not saying to you that one of these days He is going to heal your deformed child or open your blind eyes or stretch out your crooked legs — if you will just keep on praying and believing.

No, that isn't what He said to me at all. In no uncertain terms He said in a strong, powerful voice, *"How long are you going to put up with those growths on your daughter's body?"*

I was so scared I didn't know what to say. I was afraid of even being there. When you are in the presence of God, you realize how holy, how awesome He is. So just being there in the presence of the Almighty and hearing Him speak to me was enough to put the fear of the Lord into me.

Also, it was a strange feeling to be having an out-of-body experience. It's weird to know that your body is standing in your living room and yet your spirit is some place totally different.

I was so shook up I didn't know how to answer Him when He asked me what I was going to do to remove those growths. Finally, I said, "But they're not on me, Lord! I don't have them, Jesus!"

Without wasting any time, God told me, "You're the head of your house! You can curse those growths in My name just like I cursed the fig tree. If you believe and don't doubt, they will die and disappear."

The passage of Scripture the Lord used with me was Matthew 21:19-22.

> **And when he [Jesus] saw a fig tree in the way, he came to it, and found nothing thereon, but leaves only, and said unto it, Let no fruit grow on thee henceforward for ever. And presently the fig tree withered away.**
>
> **And when the disciples saw it, they marvelled, saying, How soon is the fig tree withered away!**
>
> **Jesus answered and said unto them, Verily I say unto you, If ye have faith, and doubt not, ye shall not only do this which is done to the fig tree, but also if ye shall say unto this mountain, Be thou removed, and be thou cast into the sea; it shall be done.**
>
> **And all things, whatsoever ye shall ask in prayer, believing, ye shall receive.**

Notice in verse 21 He says, **If ye have faith....** You must have faith and doubt not.

He gave me Mark 11:23 and said to me, "There is a mountain in your life — talk to it! Tell it what you want done, and it will obey you, if you do it in My name. Curse the roots of those growths, and they will have no choice but to wither and die and disappear — if you believe and not doubt."

All I could say was, "Yes, Lord," and then I began to slip back into my own body.

When I returned, immediately I went to my daughter and began to curse those growths in Jesus' name. Then for about a month, I kept believing and refusing to doubt.

One day my daughter came home from high school, still with the ugliest hands of anyone there. She went into her room to hang up some dresses. She was reaching back and forth, picking up one dress at a time and hanging it in the closet. All this time her hands were still splitting open and bleeding.

Suddenly as she reached to pick up another dress, she looked down and said, "Oh!"

She came running down the hall, bumping into the walls, holding up her hands and crying, "Daddy! Daddy! This scares me! This is spooky! Look at me! I have a new body! I have new skin — all over!"

Well, I knew it was going to happen sooner or later, I just didn't know when. The reason I knew it was going to happen was because the Lord had told me it would happen if I would believe and not doubt. And I had refused to doubt.

Here is the truth: whether you accept it or not is up to you. The truth is that if there is anything that God has promised you that you have not yet received, it is because of your dumb doubting. Now I say dumb because that's what doubting is. It's just plain stupid to doubt God.

Did you know that it takes just as much effort to doubt God as it does to believe God? Why don't we humans turn our faith loose on what God says? Why don't we trust Him and believe Him?

If you want God to work miracles in your life, then have faith in Him and His Word. Make up your mind that no matter what He says to you, you are going to *believe and not doubt!*

Confession Brings Possession

Death and life are in the power of the tongue: and they that love it shall eat the fruit thereof.

Proverbs 18:21

From that experience I learned that confession brings possession.

Remember, God spoke the entire universe into existence, and you and I have the same power to speak His

Word and see it come to pass in our lives — if we will believe and not doubt.

You know, your whole life is controlled by your tongue. If you will make up your mind to zero in on God's Word and believe exactly what He says to you, then you can receive everything that He has promised you.

"Do you really believe that works?"

I know it works!

"Did you really believe God for new hands for your daughter?"

Yes, I did.

"If I believed God for new hands, would I get them?"

Only if you refused to doubt!

If you want to see the Lord perform miracles in your life, then you must come to the place that you totally refuse to doubt anything that He says. The stronger you become in your determination to believe and not doubt, the more miracles God will perform for you. And the miracles He performs for you will be so quick and so easy.

One moment my daughter had ugly hands and ugly arms and ugly legs, and the next moment she had brand new hands and arms and legs, the prettiest in school. All those horrible growths disappeared at once. She had beautiful new skin all over her body — instantly!

That's why I am as wild as I am! Once you see God do something like that, you can never be the same again. Once you have had such an experience, it stays with you for a lifetime. You don't need to see two or three miracles like that, one is enough. You have no trouble believing God for anything after that. That's why I say that God is a miracle-working God. And what He did for me, He will do for anyone who will believe and not doubt.

What You Believe and Speak Will Determine Your Destiny

...if thou shalt confess with thy mouth..., and shalt believe in thine heart..., thou shalt be saved.

Romans 10:9

"Brother Norvel, I have a deformed child. I've been going to church for fifteen years, and the child has not been made normal yet."

That's not the way you get a deformed child made normal. You have to show the Lord that you believe and not doubt.

I know a woman who spoke to her deformed child's body for three years saying, "In Jesus' name, I command you, be normal! I'm not giving you any choice, you can't stay like this! In Jesus' name, be normal!"

You see, if you give that crooked leg a choice, it will never obey you. If you keep silent about that blind eye, it will never open. If blind Bartimaeus, who sat by the side of the road begging, had kept his mouth shut, as the crowd told him to do, he would never have been healed and would have died blind. (Mark 10:46-52.)

You have to know what causes the Lord to work miracles. If you don't know, then you won't experience the miraculous in your life. You will just live out your days in the natural. You will suffer along in God's permissive will until you die. But if you will listen to what the Lord says to you, then do it, you can have whatever you say — if you believe and do not doubt.

Your tongue is like the steering wheel on your car. Whichever way you turn the wheel, that's the way the car is going to go. In the same way, what you believe in your heart and confess with your mouth determines what the Lord is going to be able to do for you. You believed in your heart and confessed with your mouth for the salvation of your soul, so why not believe in your heart and confess with your mouth for salvation from whatever is troubling you right now?

God Rewards Faith

> **But without faith it is impossible to please him; for he that cometh to God must believe that he is, and that he is a rewarder of them that diligently seek him.**
>
> **Hebrew 11:6**

Now you may be thinking, "Well, I believed the Lord and I asked for something in prayer, but it didn't work."

Don't say that. That shows a lack of faith in God, and the Bible says that without faith it is impossible to please Him or to receive anything from Him.

If you want God to work miracles in your life, then you must have faith in Him and in His Word, regardless of what may have happened in the past to you or to those you love.

The Faith Basis

One time in a Full Gospel Business Men's convention in Indianapolis, Indiana, a lady stopped me just as I came off the platform. She had heard me speak, and she was fit to be tied. She said to me boldly, "Mr. Hayes, I don't believe what you teach!"

Now that surprised me because no one had ever told me that before. I always try to stick to the Scriptures when I teach, so I asked her, "You mean you don't believe the Bible?"

"Sure, I believe the Bible," she answered.

"Are you saying I taught something that isn't in the Bible?" I asked. "My sister, if you'll just tell me what it was, I'll repent to God, and then I'll repent to you for leading you astray. Now tell me, what did I teach this afternoon that isn't in the Bible?"

"Well," she said, "I don't know about that. All I know is that what you teach doesn't work."

"Oh, you mean the Bible doesn't work?" I asked.

"All I know is that my husband died at forty-one years of age," she answered, "and he believed that the Lord was going to heal him, right up until he took his last breath. I believed it too. And our neighbors believed it. We had thousands of Christians praying for him, and they believed it too — but he died anyway."

I could tell that she was really upset. She was only about thirty-seven or thirty-eight years old and had just lost her husband to cancer. She had asked every pastor and Full-Gospel preacher she knew to pray, and they had all prayed and prayed and believed and believed. But her husband still died — and she was angry about it.

"Well," I explained to her, "as long as you believe that the Lord is *going* to heal you, you always die. The Lord's not *going* to do anything, He has already done it. You have to accept that on a faith basis."

"What do you mean?"

"I mean, did your husband ever talk to his cancer?"

"What?"

"Did you ever hear your husband hold a conversation with his cancer?"

I could tell that she didn't understand what I was talking about, so I got out my Bible and read Mark 11:23 to her:

> **For verily I say unto you, That whosoever shall *say* unto this mountain, Be thou removed, and be thou cast into the sea; and shall not doubt in his heart, but shall believe that those things which he *saith* shall come to**

pass; he shall have whatsoever he *saith*."

"There's your answer," I told her.

"I don't see it."

So I had her read it herself several times. Finally, after reading it about five or six times she began to break down and cry.

Always remember this, my dear brother or sister in Christ: if you do not obey the Word, it may cost you your life, too. God will manifest His Word on your behalf if you will believe Him and not doubt, and if you will speak to the mountains of problems.

Faith Is the Key to Miracles

He sent his word, and healed them, and delivered them from their destructions.

Psalm 107:20

In this passage the Lord is saying to us, "I have sent My Word and My Spirit to perform miracles for you." And He will do anything for us. But we have to know how to get Him to do it.

We saw before that the first thing we must do for the Lord to work miracles for us is to worship Him continually. That does not mean every minute of the day, but it does mean on a continual basis. We said that when we spend time worshipping God, we find favor with Him.

Now in this chapter we are saying that in order to get the Lord to perform miracles on our behalf, we have got to have faith in Him and His Word.

I hear people say, "Well, a terrible thing happened to my loved one who was such a good Christian; I guess it was just God's will." The Bible is God's will! It's not fair to judge God by circumstances that are outside of His revealed will.

I have told you about my daughter and those horrible

growths on her body. Was it God's will for her to have those growths all over her body? No! God doesn't make deformed children, but He does make deformed children normal.

"Have you ever seen Him do that?"

Yes, for those who have faith in Him and in His Word.

God doesn't respond to us because of someone else's faith. He responds to each of us according to our own personal faith.

Do you need a miracle from God? Then you can get one. Remember the lady I told you about who for three years commanded her deformed child to be normal in the name of Jesus? One night as she was in bed asleep, suddenly she heard a noise in the other room. She got up to go check on her son and found that he was perfectly normal!

"Do you think that could happen to my child?"

Your deformed child can get his body straightened out if you can get your mind and mouth straightened out. But most people aren't willing to change their way of thinking. They absolutely refuse to talk to mountains. They refuse to talk to sickness and disease. They refuse to talk to deformed children and command them to be normal in the name of Jesus. They won't talk to crooked legs or blind eyes — so nothing changes.

If you have a mountain in your life — talk to it! Tell it to remove itself and be cast into the sea, in Jesus' name!

That's what I did with those growths on my daughter's body. I cursed them in the name of Jesus and told them to depart. But after I had done that, I had to believe and not doubt.

If you will do that, I am telling you that God will come to your house just as He came to mine and will make your child normal.

"Do you really think so?"

No, I don't *think* so, I *know* so!

"But miracles never happen in my house or even in my church."

No, they won't happen anywhere unless people believe God will perform them. If you want the Lord to work miracles for you, then you are going to have to recognize Him as a Miracle-Worker. You have to open your mouth without shame and call Him that.

You have to be convinced the Lord will do what He says He will do. You can't be lackadaisical in your faith. If you are, nothing will happen. God doesn't work miracles for you if you spend all your time watching football games or soap operas; He works miracles while you are exercising active faith in Him and in His Word.

Faith Moves Mountains

> **Jesus answered and said unto them, Verily I say unto you, If ye have faith, and doubt not, ye shall not only do this which is done to the fig tree, but also if ye shall say unto this mountain, Be thou removed, and be thou cast into the sea; it shall be done.**
>
> **And all things, whatsoever ye shall ask in prayer, believing, ye shall receive.**
>
> **Matthew 21:21,22**

How can you get the Lord to work miracles for you? You believe God and obey His Word.

In this passage, we see that right after He had cursed the fig tree that withered and died, Jesus said, "If you have faith and doubt not, you can command a mountain to move and be cast into the sea, and it will obey you."

Here Jesus is talking to you personally. Do you have faith to take Him at His Word and be obedient to do what

He says to do? Do you have faith to believe God? If you do, you can receive. If you don't, then you won't receive. It's just that simple.

We have seen from Romans 10:17 that faith comes by hearing, and hearing by the Word of God. In Matthew 21:21,22 Jesus says, "*If* you have faith, and doubt not, then you can have whatever you say." So not everyone has faith in what God can do. But those who do have faith can have *whatever* they ask for without doubting when it is in agreement with God's will and plan for them.

"All things..."

Notice the first three words in Matthew 21:22: **And *all* things....** That phrase "all things" included those growths on my daughter's body. It includes your deformed child. It includes your crooked leg. It includes your broken marriage. It includes your bankrupt business. It includes everything you need. If it doesn't, then Jesus lied when He said "all things."

Notice the "s" on the word "things." The Lord told me to point that out because He said that if I didn't, you might get the idea that your case is too hard for Him, or that it is not His will for you to receive what you need from Him. He told me to tell you that *whatever* your need, He can and will meet that need if you can only believe and not doubt.

Jesus plainly says that whatever you ask for in prayer (in line with God's Word), believing, you *will* receive. There are no conditions to this promise. If you put conditions on God's Word, you are operating in doubt and unbelief.

All the promises of the Bible are rightfully yours: salvation of your soul, baptism in the Holy Spirit, healing in your body, prosperity in your business, a successful marriage, obedient children, a happy home. It doesn't make any difference what kind of miracle you need; God can and will provide it for you when you believe what He says in His Word. He is a miracle-working God. He is a faith-God. He will do whatever you have faith for Him to do.

And even faith is a gift that comes by hearing God's Word. (Rom. 10:17.) Accept it as a gift from God provided through the Lord Jesus Christ for the Church.

Faith is a gift. Healing is a gift. Miracles are a gift. All these are gifts given by God to the Church, the Body of Christ, to be used for His glory.

The Gift of Healing

But the manifestation of the Spirit is given to every man to profit withal.

For to one is given by the Spirit the word of wisdom; to another the word of knowledge by the same Spirit;

To another faith by the same Spirit; to another the gifts of healing by the same Spirit.

1 Corinthians 12:7-9

One night I was speaking in a church in Baton Rouge, Louisiana, when suddenly a young girl stood up in the back of the congregation. There was a bit of a stir around her, so I asked what was going on and someone told me that a crippled girl had just risen to her feet.

"Really?" I said, "Have her come up here to the front."

So a girl about fourteen years old came down the aisle trembling and crying. There was a boy about fifteen or sixteen with her.

"This is my crippled sister," he said. "I take her everywhere." He just kept looking at her legs and saying over and over, "She's my crippled sister; I help her to go everywhere."

The little girl was still trembling and crying, so I said to her, "What happened to you, honey?"

"I don't know," she said. "I was just sitting there listening to you teach the Bible. All of a sudden something warm began to go through my crooked legs and my body. It turned from warm to hot, and I felt power go through me, down through my legs and my joints. When I felt that power, I tried to stand up on my own. I put my arms down on the side of the seat and started pushing up. When I did, I stood up and looked down, and I was totally normal."

In the New Testament that is called a gift of healing and is a function or operation of the Holy Spirit.

The Gift of the Working of Miracles

> **To another the working of miracles; to another prophecy; to another discerning of spirits; to another divers kinds of tongues; to another the interpretation of tongues.**
>
> **1 Corinthians 12:10**

Another gift of the Spirit is called the working of miracles.

We read about this kind of gift in the Old Testament when the prophet Elijah made a lost axe head "swim." (2 Kings 6:1-7.) Now we all know that axe heads don't float, so it is obvious that a miracle was involved when Elijah threw a stick into the water and the axe head rose up to the top and stayed there long enough for the worker who had lost it to pick it up.

In the New Testament we have an example of the working of miracles when Jesus fed more than five thousand people with just five little loaves of bread and two little fish. (Luke 9:12-17.)

If you will remember, when Jesus saw the multitudes that had followed Him out into the wilderness and who had brought no food with them, He tried to get the disciples to feed them. (v. 13.) But, of course, they didn't have the faith to do that. They said to Him, "But, Lord, You know we don't have but two little fish and five little barley loaves; how in the world do You expect us to feed all these people with just that?" (author's paraphrase.)

Any time God promises you something and you say to Him, "*But*, Lord..." you are operating in doubt and unbelief. Hebrews 11:6 tells us that without faith it is impossible to please God and that we must believe that He is and that He rewards those who diligently seek Him.

"But" is a conditional word, and placing conditions on the Word of God is dangerous. It can cost you your business or your marriage or your children or even your life.

What did Jesus do in this situation? He told the disciples to hand Him the loaves and fish. Then He looked up into heaven (which is where all help comes from), asked God's blessing upon them and turned to feed a crowd of more than five thousand people with still nothing in His hands but enough lunch for a few people!

That took faith! The same kind of faith that the woman showed who confessed for three long years over her deformed child that he was normal when anyone could plainly see in the natural realm that he wasn't.

Then Jesus began to break those five little loaves and two little fish and hand the pieces to His disciples to give to the hungry crowd. In fact, He did that twice. On this occasion He fed five thousand people and had twelve baskets full after it was all over. (Luke 9:17.) Another time He fed four thousand with seven loaves and a few fish and still had seven baskets full left over. (Matt. 15:32-38.)

These are two excellent examples of the working of miracles. In the New Testament there are hundreds of miracles. And they were all done through faith.

Spiritual Gifts in the Old Testament

And the mother of the child said, As the Lord liveth, and as thy soul liveth, I will not leave thee. And he arose, and followed her.

2 Kings 4:30

All but two of the nine gifts of the Spirit we have just looked at in 1 Corinthians 12:8-10 operated also in the Old Testament. Only the gifts of tongues and interpretation of tongues were not operative in Old Testament days. Because God loved the human race so much, He allowed the other seven gifts to function even before the coming of the Holy Spirit.

One of these gifts is demonstrated in 2 Kings 4:8-37 in the story of the prophet Elisha and the Shunammite woman. (My paraphrased version follows.)

This woman, a handmaid of the Lord, would always feed Elisha when he passed through her area. One day she said to her husband, "You know, Elisha is a man of God, and I want to bless him. Let's build a room for him onto our house so he will have a place to stay when he travels through here."

So they built the room for the prophet who sometimes brought with him his helper, Gehazi.

One day while the two were there, Elisha said to Gehazi, "This woman has done so much for me, I want to do something nice for her. Go ask her what she wants."

Gehazi answered, "You know, her husband is old, and she has no child."

"Go call her," said Elisha.

When the woman came in, Elisha told her, "I know you want a child, but you think you're barren. About this time next year you will have a son."

So before the child was ever conceived, the man of God spoke it into existence, because this woman was so obedient to the Lord.

About a year later, the child was born just as Elisha had prophesied. Later, when he was about thirteen years old, the boy went out to the field with his father. While he was there he had a terrible headache, and his father told one of his servants, "Take him back to his mother."

When they got back to the house, his mother held him on her lap until about noon, when he died. Then she went and laid him on the bed of Elisha, shut the door and asked her husband to let her take a servant to go along with her to meet the man of God. When he asked her why she wanted to go see the prophet, she said, **It shall be well** (v. 23).

When Elisha saw her coming a long way off, he told Gehazi, "Go meet her and ask her three things: ask her if she is well, if her husband is well, and if her son is well."

So Gehazi went and asked her these three questions, and she answered, **It is well** (v. 26).

Now this woman knew that her son had been dead for several hours. Yet she had faith enough to say that everything was well. She knew then what Jesus said later, that if she was to receive a miracle from God she had to believe and not doubt. She did just what I did when I stood in faith against those growths on my daughter's body and believed that they were cursed and would disappear.

When the woman came to Elisha, she rushed up to him and caught him by the feet, so Gehazi started to drag her away. But Elisha said to him, "Leave her alone. She's vexed in her soul, and the Lord has hidden from me the reason for it."

When Elisha found out what had happened, he gave his staff to Gehazi and sent him to the woman's house with instructions to place the staff on the boy's face. Then the woman told Elisha, "No matter what you say, I'm not leaving you until you come and do something for my boy."

So Elisha got up and followed her home. He went in to his room, shut the door and lay down on top of the boy. He put his mouth on the boy's mouth, his eyes upon the boy's eyes and his hands upon the boy's hands. In a little while the boy sneezed seven times and opened his eyes. So Elisha called for the woman and gave her back her son, alive.

Then she fell at his feet and worshipped and praised the Lord for the gift of her son's healing.

Why was this woman's child restored to life? Because she believed and did not doubt, because she kept her confession in line with what she wanted to happen and because she absolutely refused to take no for an answer.

If you want the Lord to work a miracle for you, that is exactly what you are going to have to do: believe and not doubt, keep your confession in line with what you have asked for in prayer and absolutely refuse to take no for an answer!

Speak to Your Mountain!

As I travel around the country holding meetings, many times people come to me and tell me that one of my books or tapes saved their lives. That is what the Lord called me to do, to teach His children how to live and not die, how to enjoy the abundant life that His Son gave His life to provide for them.

And one of the most important ways to do that is by talking.

When the Lord called me and told me to teach people to *talk,* I didn't know what He meant.

"They don't talk to their mountains," He explained. "Anything in their life that is causing them heartache or trouble or defeat is a mountain, and the devil put it there. I have plainly told them again and again that if anyone will say to his mountain, 'Be thou removed from me, and be thou cast into the depths of the sea,' and does not doubt but believes that what he says will come to pass, it will be done for him."

Then the Lord went on to say, "But the problem is that My children don't talk to their mountains. They go to church and listen to sermons, but they obey very little of what they hear. So I want you to teach them to talk to mountains, to empty pocketbooks, to sick bodies, to confused minds, to lost children."

God Works With Words

> **For he that speaketh in an unknown tongue speaketh not unto men, but unto God: for no man understandeth him; howbeit in the spirit he speaketh mysteries....**
>
> **He that speaketh in an unknown tongue edifieth himself....**
>
> **1 Corinthians 14:2,4**

If there is a mountain in your life, God is not going to remove it for you; you have to remove it yourself by speaking to it in the name of Jesus. When you claim something in Jesus' name, God's power does the work. But that power won't come down and do the work unless you do your part by speaking forth the Word of God in faith and confidence.

Some people tell me, "Oh, I think I'm just going to wait and see what God does about my situation."

If you just wait to see what God is going to do, you will end up dead. You are not going anywhere but to the grave. If you want out of that situation you are in, then you are going to have to do something about it yourself by putting God's power to work.

If you have a cancer that is destroying your body, then you had better start talking to it. Cancer doesn't obey your desires; it obeys your voice when you speak God's Word. The devil doesn't obey wishes; he obeys commands spoken with authority in the name of Jesus.

Remember this important principle: *God works with words!* That's what Psalm 107:20 means when it says that **He sent his word, and healed them, and delivered them from their destructions.**

Today as you are reading this book, God is saying to you, "I have sent My Word to heal you. I have sent My Word to give you instruction whereby you and your household may be saved. I have sent My Word to instruct you how to be baptized in the Holy Spirit and speak in an unknown tongue. The reason I want you to speak in an unknown tongue is because when you do so, you speak directly to Me and no one can understand you. The second reason I want you to speak in an unknown tongue is to edify yourself, to build yourself up."

After the Lord has given you His perfect instructions, if you still *can't* speak to your mountain and command it to be cast into the depths of the sea, it's because you don't have enough faith. If you *won't* speak to your mountain, it's because you are a disobedient, rebellious Christian; anyone who refuses to obey the Lord is in rebellion against Him.

No one in the world can help you but God. Your only hope is the Lord. He has more wisdom and knowledge and sense than the whole world put together. His thoughts are as much higher than a man's thoughts as the heavens are higher than the earth. (Isa. 55:9.) When your whole life is at stake, why would you refuse to listen to Him or be obedient to Him?

In your desperate situation, why would you not want to do what God says? And what He says to do is to speak to your mountain in the name of Jesus and command it to be removed from you and to be cast into the sea.

Call Things That Are Not As Though They Were

...God...calleth those things which be not as though they were.

Romans 4:17

In this verse we read that God calls those things that are not as though they were. If you want to overcome the mountains in your life, this is what you are going to have to learn to do. You will have to learn to call those things that are not, as though they were according to the Word.

In Joel 3:10, we read, **...let the weak say, I am strong**. If you are weak, why not start calling yourself strong? If you are ill, why not start calling yourself well. If you are sickly, why not call yourself healthy?

What you are calling yourself may not look true in the earthly realm, but it's true in the heavenly realm. If you want God to heal you, then you are going to have to start speaking His truth and not the world's truth.

You are not going to get God to heal you through lazy or nonchalant faith. God does not honor weak faith; He only honors strong faith. If you quote His Word with powerful faith, He will honor that Word in your life.

This same principle holds true in other areas besides health. If you are broke, for example, start calling yourself prosperous. Start praising God for blessing you financially. If you will start calling Jesus your financial Provider, I guarantee you that in six months to a year you won't be the same person.

Whatever your situation, start calling things that are not as though they were. Quote the Word of God over that situation, and sooner or later you will see it become just the way you have described it. Why? Because God has promised that His Word will not come back to Him void, but it will accomplish what it is sent to accomplish. (Isa. 55:11.)

Keep the Word in Your Mouth and in Your Heart

...The word is nigh thee, even in thy mouth, and in thy heart: that is, the word of faith, which we preach.

Romans 10:8

If you go around saying that you are sick and weak and broke and defeated, then you are in rebellion against the Word of the Lord.

If you are not feeling very well, don't call up all your friends and tell them you are sick. If you keep on doing that, you will end up dead, and they will have to come and bury you.

"But, Brother Norvel, I'm just telling the truth; I *am* sick!"

You're telling earthly truth, but a heavenly lie. You are calling yourself the way you are right now, which is rebellion against the Word of the Lord. Do as God does and begin to call things, not as they are in the natural realm, but as they are in the spiritual realm.

Do you know what I do when someone is brought to one of my meetings so weak he can't walk? I get someone to help me — we get him up and start moving him back and forth across the floor confessing, "I am strong and not weak — I am strong and not weak." Then I have him start saying it after me, over and over, "I am strong and not weak — I am strong and not weak."

How long do I do that? Until God comes and makes it so.

If you have faith to do that long enough, I guarantee you that sooner or later God will come on the scene and make it so for you too. The longer you confess the Word of God, the stronger you will get.

Never show the devil an ounce of weakness. If Satan can detect any kind of weakness in your voice at all, he will whip you.

God honors and respects and works miracles in response to strong faith, not weak faith. God does not work through weakness, He works through strength. It is the devil who works through weakness. Satan himself is a weakling and a liar. But not God. God is a God of power and truth, and He will give you that power and truth if you will show Him that you believe Him and His Word.

To do that, you must keep His Word continually in your mouth and in your heart, because your mind will fight you every step of the way. You have to learn to bypass your mind and go straight to your spirit.

Stand firm against your weakness and sickness and disease in the name of Jesus. Command it to depart from you and to be cast into the depths of the sea. Keep confessing with your mouth and believing in your heart that you are strong and not weak — and sooner or later you will be.

Be Fully Persuaded

> **Therefore it is of faith, that it might be by grace; to the end the promise might be sure to all the seed; not to that only which is of the law, but to that also which is of the faith of Abraham; who is the father of us all....**
>
> **Who against hope believed in hope, that he might become the father of many nations, according to that which was spoken, So shall thy seed be.**
>
> **And being not weak in faith, he considered not his own body now dead, when he was about an hundred years old, neither yet the deadness of Sarah's womb:**

> **He staggered not at the promise of God through unbelief; but was strong in faith, giving glory to God;**
>
> **And being fully persuaded, that what he had promised, he was able also to perform.**
>
> **Romans 4:16,18-21**

Do you really believe that the Lord has promised you divine health in His Word? Do you really believe that God has promised you financial prosperity in His Word? Do you really believe that God has promised you the salvation and blessing of your children in His Word?

Do you believe God the way Abraham believed God? According to this passage, Abraham was "fully persuaded" of what the Lord had told him. Are you *fully* persuaded of what God has told you?

If not, let me encourage you to believe fully, not in part, but fully.

"But some days I just don't feel like believing."

That kind of weak, unstable faith will put you in an early grave.

If you want the Lord to perform miracles in your life, then you must learn to do what Abraham did and stagger not at the promise of God through unbelief, but be strong in faith, giving glory to God. You must become fully persuaded that what the Lord has promised, He is able to perform — and *will* perform — not just for others, but for *you*, too.

Prosper for the Sake of the Kingdom

> **Beloved, I wish above all things that thou mayest prosper and be in health, even as thy soul prospereth.**
>
> **3 John 2**

One time I asked God, "Lord, why have You prospered me so much financially?"

"Because you passed My test," He said.

"Passed Your test? How did I pass Your test?"

"You passed My test because your soul prospered."

"Lord, do You mean to tell me that if a person's soul prospers to the point that he pleases You, then You bless him financially?"

"You got it."

Now the Bible teaches that, but the Church doesn't believe it.

The Lord went on to tell me that He blesses not only with money, but with health. He told me, "I do that because I want My children to be able to serve Me and to pay their bills and keep a good name."

If that is true, and it is, then why do we in the Church not believe it? If we will learn to prosper our souls, then our bodies and our finances will also prosper. Then we will be able to do what the Lord has put us on this earth to do — win the world to Christ.

If you want the Lord to perform miracles for you and your family so that you can be a blessing to others, then worship Him in spirit and in truth — and have faith in Him and in His Word.

3
Miracles Come Through *Work* — Putting Your Faith in Action

3
Miracles Come Through *Work* — Putting Your Faith in Action

> **And God hath set some in the church, first apostles, secondarily prophets, thirdly teachers, after that miracles, then gifts of healings, helps, governments, diversities of tongues.**
>
> **1 Corinthians 12:28**

In this chapter we will be looking at this one verse, but oh, what a powerful verse it is! I believe I could teach on it for a month.

The reason I am devoting an entire chapter to this one verse is because I want you to see and understand the very special gifts that the Lord has set in His Church, **For the perfecting of the saints, for the work of the ministry, for the edifying of the body of Christ** (Eph. 4:12).

Each of these gifts represents an office or a work that is done by individual members of the Body of Christ. When a person fulfills his office or carries out his work well, he will be promoted by God (Luke 19:17), just as his hard work will bring him promotion in the world.

Work Brings Promotion

In the introduction to this book I told how I rose from salesman to executive in a manufacturing firm. I did that while still in my twenties, which is very unusual. I was able to do it for two reasons: 1) because I just happened to have great knowledge of that particular business, and 2) because I worked very hard. When you are good at something, people will promote you. When I was a teenager I worked for a supermarket chain. I went in two hours early every day to get my department cleaned up and ready for the day. The night watchman told the manager of the store about me, and the manager called me into the office and said to me, "Don't tell any of the other employees, but I'm going to give you a raise because you do such good work and keep your department so clean."

It wasn't long before the manager told the district supervisor about me. One day the supervisor called me into the office and said, "I know you're only nineteen or twenty years old, and it's against company policy to make anybody a store manager before the age of twenty-four, but I just want you to know that if you'll stay with us, I'll do everything I can to get you a manager's position as soon as possible."

That taught me a lesson. Early in life I learned that in the world, hard work brings promotion. I have since learned that the same is true in the Kingdom of God.

God Promotes Faithfulness

> **...He which soweth sparingly shall reap also sparingly; and he which soweth bountifully shall reap also bountifully.**
>
> **2 Corinthians 9:6**

If you will work, God will promote you — even if you're not saved — because it's part of God's law to promote faithfulness.

One time I worked with a businessman, a sinner, who had started out with nothing, and in twelve years God had made him a millionaire. He told me, "You know, I have given a lot of money to God. I send money to the 700 Club. I watch it on TV, and I believe it's a good thing to send money to programs like that."

Then he went on to tell me, "I send money to other TV preachers. I send those people money because I have so much coming in that I just can't spend it all on myself. I started off with hardly any business at all, and now my business is worth a million dollars."

And this man wasn't even saved.

"I pray and ask God to help me," he said. "I give my money to Him, and He helps me."

"Do you know Him?" I asked.

"No, I don't know Him."

"Are you living in sin?"

"Yeah, I'm living in sin. But I give the Lord a lot of money, and you know, He helps me make more."

Then he looked at me and asked, "Doesn't God love everybody?"

"Oh, you said that right." I told him, and then I spent four hours talking to him and leading him to the Lord.

"Brother Norvel, do you mean that God blesses sinners?"

Sure, if they give to Him and His work. Remember, the principle is, "Freely give, freely receive." That's a divine law — and it works for anybody who will live by it.

The Power of the Spirit

I have seen a sick sinner come into a service and sit down beside a sick believer. As the Word of God is preached, all of a sudden the power of the Holy Spirit goes forth and begins to heal the sick Christian. Then just as suddenly the sick sinner begins to get healed too.

Why does that happen? It happens because the sinner is in the right place at the right time. The healing power of the

Holy Spirit jumps from the believer to the sinner and does the same work in his body that it did in the believer's body.

The healing power of God is an enemy to all disease, and when that power is manifested, it will attack any sickness it comes in contact with.

That's why if you will confess the Word of God the way you are supposed to, the Holy Spirit will manifest Himself in you — because the Spirit and the Word agree.

If you are sick, confess healing verses. Don't confess other Scriptures. If you confess the Word of God over your sickness, the Holy Spirit will confirm the Word and will agree with you as you claim your healing in the name of Jesus. The Spirit will manifest Himself to you, and the healing power of God will go to work within you, because you are coming into agreement with the Word of God.

God doesn't have any pets. (Acts 10:34.) He will manifest Himself to anyone who will believe His Word in his heart and confess it with his lips. (Rom. 10:9,10.)

Believe According to the Word

You can have the Holy Spirit within you for twenty-five years and still never receive anything from the Lord. How much He works for you depends on how much faith you have, how much of His Word you believe with your heart and confess with your mouth.

You can't believe just anything and get blessed by God. You have to believe according to His Word.

The Bible says that God is not willing that any should perish, but that all should come to a saving knowledge of the Lord Jesus Christ. (2 Pet. 3:9.) The same Bible says that God wills above all things that we prosper and be in health, even as our soul prospers. (3 John 2.) God doesn't want anybody to be sick or poor, any more than He wants them to be lost.

It is so important to get it firmly established in your mind and heart that God wants to bless you in every way. But it is just as important to remember that whatever the Lord does for you depends upon what you believe in your heart and confess with your mouth.

Listen and Obey

I say that Jesus Christ is the best businessman I ever met. That is part of my daily confession. I walk the floor saying, "Lord Jesus, You are the best businessman I know. You won't let me make a bad investment. You'll show me where to put my money so that it will produce a good return. If I start to make an investment that is unwise, You'll grieve my spirit so that I back away from it."

That's the way you ought to pray before you make any big decision like investing money, changing jobs, or getting married. I have known people who wished they had prayed that kind of prayer for wisdom and guidance before they got married. If they had, they would have missed a lot of misery.

Someone once asked me, "Brother Norvel, do you pray the same prayer about marriage that you do about business investments?"

I sure do. That's the reason I am still single. Sometimes I wish the Holy Spirit would say to me, "Go get 'em!" But unless He says so, I am not going anywhere. I will just sit in my rocking chair and praise God. I would rather be ninety-five years old and still sitting and rocking back and forth with a free mind and heart, praising the Lord, than to be in a marriage that is not the will of God.

If you will listen to the Holy Spirit, He will guide you and counsel you so that you don't make foolish mistakes like marrying the wrong person.

One time the Lord told me, "Norvel Hayes, in your life you will make a lot of mistakes."

"Oh, God, don't remind me," I said. "I've made so many mistakes already that I feel like a flake!"

"But remember," He said, "the Holy Ghost lives inside of you, and He doesn't make mistakes. Listen to Him and obey Him. Go wherever He wants you to go and do whatever He wants you to do."

That's good advice for anybody.

The Ministry Gifts

> **And God hath set some in the church, first apostles, secondarily prophets, thirdly teachers, after that miracles, then gifts of healings, helps, governments, diversities of tongues.**
>
> **1 Corinthians 12:28**

Now let's examine this important verse more closely to see what the Lord would say to us through it.

First of all, notice that it is God and not man Who sets these ministry gifts in the Body.

Next, notice that God has set **some**. This tells us that God has chosen special people and appointed and anointed them for special ministries.

Finally, notice that these special ministries are ordained and instituted by God not in the world, but in His Church, the Body of Christ. Unfortunately, not all of these gifts are operative in all churches because not all churches believe, receive and exercise these gifts.

Then the verse goes on to list the ministry gifts that God has set in the Church, beginning with **apostles** and ending with **diversities of tongues**. One of these ministries is simply called **helps**. This is the one we will look at first because it is the one I was first called to by the Lord.

The Ministry of Helps

God calls people to the ministry of helps just as He calls people to the ministries of teaching or prophecy or the working of miracles. I know, because when I surrendered to the Lord I was called to this important ministry.

Now as I have told you, when I first gave my life to Jesus, as a business executive, I didn't know anything about God. All I knew was how to make money. So I went and talked to my pastor, because he knew more about God than I did.

Later on, the Lord moved me to Cleveland, Tennessee, where I came into contact with a Full-Gospel Pentecostal minister, Reverend Littlefield, who had a ministry of helps.

The way we met is interesting. He came into a restaurant I had just bought as an investment and asked me about sponsoring a radio broadcast. The Spirit of God spoke to me and said, "I want you to talk to this man." I took him into my office and gave him my testimony about the Lord coming to visit me in my car for an hour and a half.

I said, "Reverend Littlefield, I don't know much of anything about God. He has called me to follow Him and serve Him, but I need to be trained. What do I do?"

"Just obey the Lord," he said. "Do whatever He tells you to do."

This man was the first one to take me to a Full Gospel Businessmen's meeting. I was so impressed when I saw other successful businessmen get up and give their testimony about their relationship with Jesus and about working with God.

One man, the owner of a chain of department stores, stood up and told how he would look out over his store and see someone he knew only by the Spirit who was dying with cancer. He would go out and tap that person on the shoulder and say, "Would you please come into my office? I want to talk to you about your cancer."

"I don't know you. How do you know I have cancer?"

"The Lord told me so, and He wants to heal you."

"But I don't know anything about healing."

"That's all right — the Lord will teach you — if you are willing to believe and receive."

Then the businessman told how he would sit the person down in a special chair in his office, pray and lay hands on him and the Lord would heal him.

When I heard that, I began to come alive. I said to myself, "My mother died with cancer. I wish she could have found that office. But she went to a church that didn't teach about healing or hold healing services."

So I began to work with Reverend Littlefield. I worked with him for seven years in the ministry of helps. I went to his church and traveled all over the country with Full Gospel Businessmen.

One of the greatest trips I ever took was with Nicky Cruz, John Gimenez, John Sherrill and Jack Brown. We took a mission journey to London, England, where we spent two weeks working in the streets among drug addicts. That mission trip changed my whole life. Now I make such journeys often to places like Northern Ireland, Hawaii and other locations all over the globe.

Faithfulness in Helps Brings Blessing and Promotion

Whenever I talk about this subject, someone always asks me, "Brother Norvel, exactly what did you do in the ministry of helps?"

I did a lot of different things. I worked with poor children. I distributed clothes to the needy. I drove Reverend Littlefield wherever he needed to go. I went on Full Gospel Businessmen's airlifts.

When a preacher like Nicky Cruz would come to town, I would escort him around for weeks from place to place where he could witness to thousands of people. I would organize his services, introduce him in the meetings, take up offerings for him and sell his records and books.

I stayed busy doing a variety of things to help others in their ministry. And the Lord blessed me so much I could hardly stand it. It just made me want to help others even more. And the more I gave, the more I received in return.

Never underestimate the ministry of helps. God may want you to help other ministers for years before you have a ministry of your own. He had me doing that for a long time. My brother or sister, if I can walk out of an executive office and go to minister in the city dump, helping poor people in that stinking place for seven long years, then surely you can do it too. Show the Lord He can trust you, and He will make you ruler over much. (Matt. 25:23.) Seek the Lord, and He will show you great and mighty things that you know not. (Jer. 33:3.)

The Office of Teacher

After I had served in the ministry of helps for seven years, the Lord spoke to me and said, "Now I'm going to set you in the office of teacher."

Notice that in 1 Corinthians 12:28 this is the third office. First comes apostles, next prophets, and third, teachers.

When He called me to fill this office, the Lord said to me, "I want you to teach people what I have taught you."

That may happen to you one day, but in the meantime keep first things first. Be satisfied with the ministry of helps so God can train you. Just because you have a call of God on you, don't start telling the Lord, "I want to start off teaching crowds of thousands." At this stage you probably aren't qualified to teach fifty people, much less thousands.

Before He can release you into full ministry, God has to train you. Start out teaching your own family first. Then you may have a congregation of four or five people. If you are faithful in that ministry, then the Lord can promote you progressively to greater things. Remember, the Lord will promote you as He sees that He can trust you.

Now this term "teacher" doesn't refer to a Sunday school teacher. In this sense, a teacher is someone who unfolds the Word of God to others, explaining to them what the Word is and what makes it work.

For example, lately the Lord has been dealing with me about teaching His Word to cancer patients, terminal cases who have no hope. He has told me that He wants me to go to them and show them how to get healed.

So now I go into hospital rooms where people are dying of cancer, and I tell them, "You don't have to die!" I bind up that cancer in the name of Jesus. I take a Bible and sit down with them for an hour or an hour and a half. I teach them how to talk, how to take the Word of God and stand against that disease that is trying to destroy them. That is part of my ministry as a teacher.

In fact, I have made up a whole series of tapes and even written a book about this type of ministry called *How To Live and Not Die.** People have been listening to these tapes and reading this book and coming off of death beds.

I couldn't do that when I first started out in ministry. I had to be trained. I couldn't work in the ministry of helps until Reverend Littlefield trained me in it. I couldn't witness to people until the Full Gospel Businessmen trained me to go into the streets and schools and college classrooms and talk to people about the Lord Jesus Christ.

---

*See the list at the back of this book.

I had to overcome a lot of personal pride that was keeping me from learning how to flow in ministry. Once I did that, the Lord began to open to me doors of service everywhere. Now today, with the help of my team, I sow seeds all over this nation and the world because that's my God-ordained ministry — the ministry of teacher.

The Ministry of Healing

After I had been faithful in the ministry of helps and the ministry of teacher, the Lord gave me the ministry of healing.

In my meetings, I often exercise that ministry through the laying on of hands. Whenever I teach on healing, the Lord anoints my hands so I can lay them on others and they can receive their healing.

At others times the Lord will direct me to instruct people to bring me handkerchiefs and pieces of cloth so I can lay hands on them and send them back to the sick as a means of healing, as was done in Paul's day.

> **And God wrought special miracles by the hands of Paul:**
>
> **So that from his body were brought unto the sick handkerchiefs or aprons, and the diseases departed from them, and the evil spirits went out of them.**
>
> **Acts 19:11,12**

"Do you think people really get healed by placing those handkerchiefs and cloths on their sick bodies?"

I *know* they do. You should see the letters that come to our office from people who have been healed or had demons driven from them because they applied a cloth that I had laid hands on. The Lord performs mighty miracles in response to the faith that is placed in Him through the laying on of hands and the applying of handkerchiefs and cloths.

This is just one form of the healing ministry that God has given me. Another is the ministry of giving people new hearts, which I will discuss later.

Then about five years later the Lord gave me another ministry of helps. That came about in a very dramatic way.

A Second Ministry of Helps

I had been ministering in a meeting with Kenneth Hagin when I fell under the power of the Spirit and had to be carried back to my room. The next morning when I came out from under the anointing, I was lying in the bed with my eyes open, and everything was peaceful and quiet. Suddenly the wall of the motel room totally disappeared, and I saw a vision like those described in the Scriptures.

The Bible records different kinds of visions. The open vision is the highest type. This is the kind Paul experienced when he met the risen Jesus on the road to Damascus. (Acts 9:1-9.) Then there is a vision in which the person falls into a trance and sees things, as when Peter fell into a trance on the housetop and saw the vision of the sheet being let down from heaven. (Acts 10:9-16.) A night vision is one that comes in the form of a dream, as when Paul saw the man from Macedonia who said to him, **Come over into Macedonia, and help us** (Acts 16:9-12).

All types of visions are important, but the one I received was given to me when I was wide awake with my eyes open.

As the wall disappeared, I saw a hill with a tree on it. I could see the tree very clearly, and it was full of fruit, but it was so far away I couldn't tell what kind of fruit it was. Suddenly, the scene changed, and the tree was much closer to me. The fruit had fallen off of it, and I could see it lying around the trunk. As I looked closer, I saw that it was no longer fruit but money. It was piled up all around the base of the tree, about a foot and a half deep.

Then all of a sudden the scene changed again, and the tree turned into me. I saw myself standing there with money piled up all around my feet and legs. The Lord spoke to me and said, "I am calling you to bear fruit and blessings for the Body of Christ as I direct you."

Like Paul after he had met Jesus on the road to Damascus, I had no choice but to be obedient to the heavenly vision. (Acts 26:19.) So now when the Lord tells me that He wants me to do something for one of His servants — which is the ministry of helps — I do it.

Let me give you an example.

Some time ago I was staying in the home of an evangelist and was down at his swimming pool getting some exercise after a meeting. The Spirit of the Lord came upon me and said, "I want you to speak at a certain church Sunday."

That was the only time in my life I ever called a pastor and asked to take part in his service. I arranged to take up an offering in his church the next Sunday.

When I got to the church, the Lord spoke to me and said, "I want you to take up an offering for two pastors who don't have any money."

So during the course of the service I took up an offering for these pastors. Now I didn't know it, but they had no salary because they had been giving all their money to the church. Instead of having thousands of dollars, as they should have, they had nothing. One of them didn't even have enough money to take his wife and children out for Sunday dinner — and he was the Sunday morning speaker!

So when the Lord told me to take up an offering for those men, I did as I was told. After the offering was taken, the ushers brought down $6,000.

The Lord said to me, "Split it between the pastor and the assistant pastor evenly, fifty-fifty." Those two men and their wives wound up with their faces to the floor, weeping before God.

After that congregation had given their money to those men, the Lord began to move among them. People began to get healed and to dance all over the place.

God Promotes Just As He Places

So when the Lord directs me to go anywhere and do anything, I consider it part of my ministry of helps. I am called to help people who have nothing.

I knew that was my calling when I was sent as a company executive down to the city dump to help those people there. I knew it when I was sent to give out clothes to the poor and to buy food for starving families. I can still see the faces of some of those hungry children who would tear into the bags of food I brought before I could even set them down on the table because the poor little things hadn't eaten in days. I would stand there and the Spirit of God would come on me so strong and heavy I could hardly bear it.

I would rather carry food to poor houses and be in God's perfect will than to speak to the biggest crowd in the United States and be out of God's perfect will. I am not interested in anything that is in God's permissive will.

If I have learned one thing in this life, it's that it is so sweet and so blessed to be in God's perfect will.

I have also learned that when you are in the ministry, you don't have to promote yourself. In fact, God won't allow it. It is the Lord Who does the promoting of ministries just as it is the Lord Who does the setting of the ministries in the Church in the first place — as it pleases Him. If He wants you to have something, He will see that you get it, if you will just be faithful where you are and with what you have and continue to worship Him and bless others.

If you do that long enough, I guarantee you that God will start promoting you — that is, if He can trust you.

The Ministry of Tongues, of a Prophet and of an Apostle

In the teaching ministry, God requires you to teach what He has taught you. So I began to teach people the ministry of helps. Then the Lord impressed upon me that He wanted to use me in tongues, interpretation of tongues and prophecy, and those areas became a part of my ministry as well.

When the Lord first began to deal with me about this ministry, I wouldn't speak in tongues in public for two years. I only gave in and began to be fully obedient to the Lord's will after a supernatural prayer meeting one night in the home of Kenneth Hagin.

In that meeting, the gifts of prophecy, tongues and interpretation of tongues came to me, and the Lord told me that I had better yield my tongue and voice to Him. I knew that God had already told Brother Hagin, "I have set you in the office of a prophet and have told you to prophesy. If you don't do it, you are going to die in seven years."

The office of prophet is the second gift or ministry listed in 1 Corinthians 12:28. The office of the apostle is first. The word *apostle* means one sent — "he that is sent,"[1] "one sent on a mission."[2] Usually we think of it as someone who has been sent to far-off lands to build churches and to raise up ministries.

"I thought that was the work of a missionary."

---

[1]James Strong, "Greek Dictionary of the New Testament," (Nashville: Abingdon, 1890), p. 15, entry #652.

[2]*Webster's Ninth New Collegiate Dictionary*, s.v. "apostle."

Actually, the word *missionary* is not found in the *King James Bible*. Instead, the Scriptures use the word *apostle*. An apostle is one who operates in some phase of the apostolic ministry. If you are an apostle, you go wherever the Lord sends you to carry out His mission in the world.

Lester Sumrall is a typical apostle of God. The Lord can send him to a foreign country where he doesn't even know the language and tell him to build a church in the downtown area of a huge city — and somehow he will get it done.

That's called operating in the office and ministry of an apostle.

Brother Hagin, on the other hand, operates in the office and ministry of a prophet.

"What's a prophet?"

A prophet is one who receives revelation knowledge from God and then passes it on to others. Each of us may prophesy from time to time, but a prophet is one who is responsible to God to operate in this gift on a regular basis. The spirit of prophecy can come upon Brother Hagin at any time, and when it does, which is often, it just boils up out of him supernaturally.

That is what Brother Hagin was rebelling against, until the Lord came to him when he was forty-eight years old and told him that he would die by age fifty-five if he did not function in that office.

When the Lord sets you in an office of the Church, it is important that you function in that office. It doesn't matter if it's in the city dump in the ministry of helps. If that is where the Lord has set you, function there. Don't try to promote yourself. When God is pleased with you, He will promote you. It doesn't matter whether you preach or sing or play the piano, if you are faithful to operate in the office God has given you, He will promote you at the right time.

Diversities of Tongues

So several years after I had begun to yield myself to speak in tongues in public, the Lord came back and gave me a second ministry in tongues, just as He had done with the ministry of helps. This was a special tongues ministry.

The Lord would send me on special missions, like to conventions. At times He would send me to one of Oral Roberts' services and tell me in advance to get a front row seat because after Brother Roberts had spoken I was to get up and deliver a message in tongues.

"I don't want you to prophesy," the Lord would tell me, "I want you to speak the message in tongues, and somebody else will give the interpretation."

I would go and take a seat down front and just wait. About two minutes before Brother Roberts would get through with his sermon, all of a sudden a message in tongues would start to rise up out of me. As soon as Brother Roberts finished speaking, the Lord would say to me, "Go!" I would rush to the microphone and speak out in tongues the message the Lord had given me.

That is what the apostle Paul calls **diversities of tongues** in 1 Corinthians 12:28 or **divers kinds of tongues** in verse 10 of that same chapter, meaning different languages.

Sometimes the Lord will give me a message to speak in one language, and at other times the message will be in a different language. Sometimes when I speak in tongues, the Holy Ghost will laugh, and at other times He will weep. It's not me laughing or crying; it's the Holy Ghost on the inside of me Who has taken over my spirit.

Sometimes it is a power-stripping message that I am to deliver, and sometimes it is a very gentle, quiet message that comes forth from my mouth. Whatever it is, it is up to the Lord and not me.

Sometimes when I speak in tongues, the Holy Spirit will moan. At other times He will move me to dance. I never know what the Spirit is going to say or do through me, because the interpretation is not up to me; He gives that to somebody else.

I have continued to operate in the special ministry of tongues, as the Lord directs. He doesn't always give me a message to deliver in every service. And I don't go around the country trying to expose the ministry gift He has given me. I only operate in it when the Holy Spirit causes it to rise up out of me — as He wills, not as I will.

And I don't get jealous if the Lord doesn't let me operate in that gift. I know this is a divine responsibility that the Lord has placed on me, and I take it very seriously. That's the attitude you should have about whatever ministry gift the Lord chooses to bestow upon you.

The Gifts of Miracles and Healings

Notice that after the gifts of apostles, prophets, and teachers, there are the gifts of miracles and healings.

In my own ministry, the Lord has given me two or three specific kinds of miracles. More than anything else, He has given me miracles for feet, new feet. He has also given me miracles for new hearts, as I have mentioned.

The first time these miracles were manifested in my ministry was several years ago.

I was riding in a car on my way to speak at a Full Gospel Business Men's chapter meeting when all of a sudden my heart began to hurt so bad I could hardly stand it. At the meeting place, I got out of the car and made my way to the platform. All the time I was sitting there during the preliminaries, my heart was hurting, and I didn't know why. But I could hear the voice of God within me saying, "No, no, don't go back to your room."

In the natural you would think that I was having a heart attack, but instead the Lord was letting me experience the suffering of the people who were in that meeting. He was allowing me to feel their infirmities.

Just before I was introduced as the speaker for the evening, the Lord spoke to me and said, "I want you to call people down front who have bad hearts. I'm going to pop new hearts in their chests."

That was news to me. I had never heard of anything like that before. But I did as I was told and called down to the front all those who had bad hearts. The Holy Ghost took over, and those people began to fall flat on the floor. The Lord would pop a new heart into one of them, and he would just topple over and fall down.

The same kind of thing happens with feet. It is just a gift that God has given me to bring miracles in these two areas. I never know when these miracles will manifest themselves. I may go for six months without it happening, and then it may happen twice within two weeks. I never know when it's coming.

Other people have different gifts of miracles and healings.

Not too long ago, Lester Sumrall and I were holding two crusades together, one in Hong Kong and another in Manila in the Philippines. As we were sitting in Hong Kong talking with an evangelist from Oregon, Brother Sumrall said, "You know, I've got several decayed teeth in my mouth, and I'm going to have to take some time off and get some dental work done."

The evangelist said to him, "Brother Sumrall, did you know that Jesus sometimes heals people's teeth through my ministry? He has given me that gift."

Brother Sumrall came alive.

"He does?" he said.

"Yes, but He doesn't always fill all of them," said the evangelist.

That's the way it works with hearts and feet in my ministry. I would say that probably seven or eight out of every ten people get new hearts. The Lord will just come to them and pop a new heart in their chest.

So Brother Sumrall said to the evangelist, "Well, pray for me right now."

The man reached out and prayed a very simple prayer in Jesus' name, saying, "Lord, fill Lester's teeth."

Brother Sumrall opened his mouth, and all of his teeth were filled with gold!

That is a special gift, the fourth gift of the working of miracles, creative miracles.

Now that doesn't work for me, because I haven't been given the ministry of filling teeth. The Lord has given me the ministry of new hearts. I don't give people new hearts, but the Lord does it through my ministry. I don't know why He chose to use me in this way, but He did.

God has chosen to set some in the Church through whom He works miracles and healings, just as He has given some to be apostles, prophets and teachers and some as gifts of government and diversities of tongues.

Whatever gift the Lord may have chosen to bestow upon you, be faithful to function in that office. If you will do that, if you will worship the Lord, have faith in Him and do the work that He has given you to do, He will promote you and perform miracles for you and through you.

4

Miracles Come Through *Knowledge and Obedience* — God Promises Results!

4

Miracles Come Through *Knowledge and Obedience* — God Promises Results!

The thief cometh not, but for to steal, and to kill, and to destroy: I am come that they might have life, and that they might have it more abundantly.

John 10:10

Many people do not know where disease and other such evils come from. Here in this verse Jesus plainly tells us that all evil comes from the devil and that all good comes from God.

You need to get it straight in your mind and heart once and for all that *all* good things come from God. The devil has nothing good in him. He is obsessed with total destruction. He doesn't even think good. All he does day and night is sit around trying to figure out some way to get to you to do you harm.

That's why you need to have knowledge of good and evil, in order to resist him.

The Operation of Demons

Three times in my life God has taken me out of my body, just as Kenneth Copeland prophesied would happen many years ago at a convention in Jackson, Mississippi.

"The Lord God is going to manifest Himself to you three different times and show you the whole kingdom of the devil's work," he told me.

Within a period of about two or three years, the Lord took me up in the air and let me travel with demons to see how they operate. What I learned was that demons don't have much sense. All they do day and night is roam back and forth over the earth seeking whom they may devour. (See 1 Pet. 5:8.) They especially frequent bars and prostitute sections of various cities. They roam up and down the streets looking for likely prospects. Anyone who listens to them will be deceived into sin and destruction.

But you will never be possessed of the devil if you will stay off of his territory. You cannot fool around with the devil without the devil getting to you. No demon is strong enough to get in you unless you begin to think like he thinks or cooperate with him.

Devils don't have enough power over humans to force them to do anything. (And we believers have power over them.) Neither are they very smart. They are totally "flaky." They just float around in the air like chicken hawks looking down to try to find some poor, ignorant person who will listen to them.

There are all kinds of demons. There are lying demons and lustful demons and thieving demons, but none of them has anything good to think or say. All you have to do to avoid them is to stay off of their territory. Or if they try to get near you, submit yourself to God, resist the devil and he and his demons will flee. (See James 4:7.) If you will do that, your mind will stay clear and your spirit will remain strong, and you will be able to glorify the name of Jesus until the day you die.

Ignorance Brings Destruction, Knowledge Brings Miracles

My people are destroyed for lack of knowledge....

Hosea 4:6

You can't fool around with the devil without getting burned. He will attack you when you least expect it, right where you are the weakest. That's why you must always be on guard against him and his demons. You must know how to resist him and overcome him.

The same is true of churches. There are some churches that do not accept Jesus as Healer. If you listen to these people, you will be attacked by sickness or some other evil. If you do come under attack by some killer disease like cancer, and you don't know what to do about it, then you will die in your ignorance because you don't know how to resist the devil and his evil.

It's not enough just to pray and ask God to heal you. You must do something about your own situation. In order to get the Lord to perform miracles for you, you are going to have to have knowledge — you must know how to get God to work for you. As we have said, the Holy Spirit of God will perform any kind of miracle for you that you need, but He is not going to do it unless you have a knowledge of miracles.

The Lord will heal anyone, but unless you have a knowledge of healing, *you* won't be healed. You can't just lie around saying, "Oh, I've prayed, and now I'm waiting for the Lord to heal me, if it's His will."

If you do that, you won't be healed. You have to show God your faith. Just as you had to make Jesus your Savior by faith and confession, so you have to make Him your Healer by faith and confession. It takes the same kind of active faith to be healed as it does to be saved. And both of them require knowledge of the will and way of God, which comes only through knowledge of His Word.

There are some churches, like the one in which I grew up, who have strong faith for salvation. If those people ever develop the same kind of faith for healing that they have for salvation, all the doctors in town will be out of a job and all the hospitals will be empty.

These people have great faith — but it's all in one area, salvation. They don't need more faith, they just need faith in the right area. They believe that God *can* heal anybody. The problem is that they don't believe that God *will* heal anybody — even though they believe He will *save* anybody. That's why my mother died of cancer at the age of thirty-seven, and why my brother died of kidney disease at the age of nineteen. No one ever taught them to have faith for the healing of their bodies just as they were taught to have faith for the salvation of their souls.

Knowledge Produces Results

When I was seven years old, I developed a physical condition that required me to stay in bed all winter long. I couldn't go outside or even breathe cold air because the doctor told my mother that if I ever caught cold, I would die.

My mother kept me alive by heating irons to warm the bed. Then I had to watch her die of cancer two or three years later.

I know what it's like to have to stay in bed for a long period of time with nothing to do to entertain yourself. I was so bored I counted every crack in the wall. That's really hard for an active child. My brother and sister were gone to school all day, so I would get up and play in front of the fireplace.

The one good thing that came out of that time was that I learned to play marbles really well. When I first started, I couldn't hit the side of a barn. I'd try to shoot, and the marble would go any which way. But I kept practicing and practicing, and the marble began to go closer and closer to where I wanted it to go.

After several weeks of practice, I could take my "taw" and hit any marble with it I wanted. Not only would the "taw" hit the other marble and knock it out of the circle, but it would stick right there where it hit so I could get another shot.

I kneeled down and played marbles so much that my big toenail and my thumbnail both came off. Finally I got to where I could hit the marble I wanted every time and stick my "taw" right there in the same spot so I could go on playing until I had won every marble in the ring.

That's the way you have to be about the Word of God. If you don't get in the habit of reading, studying and meditating on the Bible day in and day out, you will never learn enough to know how to believe God for the good things He has promised you in His Word.

When I first started, I didn't know anything about playing marbles, just as later on I didn't know anything about God when I started serving Him. But after weeks of practice I became the school marble champion. During the next few years, I got so good that no one would play me, even though they were bigger and older than I was, because I always won. I would walk around with my pockets full of marbles. Other kids would hear them rattling together in my pockets and say, "I hear Norvel coming."

The same thing happened when I began to play pool. I developed my eye and hand coordination so that it wasn't long before I could beat my teacher. Then after a while I was competing with the hustlers. Pretty soon I was so good I couldn't get a game in town, so I started traveling around the country as a pool hustler.

When you are a pool hustler, you are treated like a movie star. You have fans and a following and a reputation. You go into a town and challenge the local hustler, and all the pool sharks and gamblers stand around and watch you play for hours. All eyes are on you.

I finally made my way to Kansas City, but when it got to where I couldn't find anybody to play me anymore, I got a job as a traveling salesman. I stopped playing pool for a living, and I haven't hustled pool since.

Later I started my own business and was very successful at it. Then, as I have already explained, I became an executive, which is what I was when God manifested Himself to me and told me that He wanted me to follow Him. That's when I met the Full-Gospel Pentecostal preacher who got me started ministering in his church.

And all of this happened because whatever I did, I developed expertise in that area. Through all these experiences I learned one important thing that you need to learn too: *knowledge produces results.*

If You Want Miracles, Get To Know the Lord!

And I will pray the Father, and he shall give you another Comforter, that he may abide with you for ever;

Even the Spirit of truth; whom the world cannot receive, because it seeth him not, neither knoweth him: but ye know him; for he dwelleth with you, and shall be in you.

John 14:16,17

Everything I ever got from God I received by grace through faith. (Eph. 2:8.) Whatever I have in my life and ministry came because the Lord gave it to me.

"What has He given you?"

Well, for one thing He has given me His healing power in my hands. It comes into manifestation every time I talk about it and read Scriptures about it. When it manifests itself and I lay hands on people, if they will believe, they are healed.

Do you know why some people find it hard to believe and trust God for their healing? It's because they don't really know Him.

A little child will not go to a stranger, but that same child will rush into the arms of its mother. Why? Because the child knows its mother. That's the way you and I have to be with our heavenly Father. We must come to know Him, because to know Him is to trust Him.

If you don't trust the Lord, it's because you don't know Him. There is no way that you can really know God and not have total trust in Him.

Now you may know the Lord as your Savior, but do you know Him as your Healer, as your Provider, as your Miracle-Worker? Are you as sure that He will manifest Himself to you and drive out the demons and the disease from your body as you are that He is your Savior and will take you to heaven when you die?

If you know that the Lord will heal you, no matter what your sickness or disease or condition, then you can receive your healing. If you don't know for sure whether He will do that for you, then it's because you don't really know Him.

God will do anything you ask Him to do for you, but to get Him to do it, you have to know Him personally. How do you get acquainted with God? You get acquainted with Him through His Word. God is not just a name, He is a Person. And the way you get to know Him is by getting to know His Word of truth. (John 17:17.) Jesus tells us that the Holy Spirit Who comes to dwell within us is the Spirit of truth and that we will know the truth, and the truth will make us free. (See John 14:16,17; John 8:32.)

So once again we see that it is knowledge — knowledge of God through His Word of truth — that causes the Lord to perform miracles for us.

Knowledge Brings Power

Some people are so ignorant of spiritual things that they don't even know where evil comes from. If you tell them that the devil is attacking them, it makes them mad, because they don't even believe in the devil.

Many people in our society today are totally demon-possessed, but if you try to tell them, they will say, "Don't say that! I am <u>not</u> possessed of the devil!" That is the demon in them talking, which is proof that they are under the control of the evil one.

Now if you are not willing to be possessed of the devil, why would you be willing to be tormented by the devil? Sickness and disease don't come from God, they come from Satan. Just as God uses knowledge to bring health and every good thing, the devil uses ignorance to bring disease and every evil thing.

If you begin to operate in ignorance or doubt or unbelief, just watch and see what happens. The devil will put some sickness on you. That's why you have to resist him in the name of Jesus. You have to take a stand against the devil and say to him, "No, you don't! I won't accept this! In the name of Jesus, you depart from me! Get out of my body right this minute!"

The greatest word you will ever say to the devil is "NO!" These are two little letters, but, oh, how powerful. If you will stand firm against the devil in the name of Jesus, you will be set free from whatever Satan tries to bring against you.

I have news for you: no matter who you are or where you live, you are going to be attacked by the devil. The reason that happens is because we are living in an imperfect world. The Bible calls Satan **the god of this world** (2 Cor. 4:4), and as long as we are living on this earth we will have to contend with him. How successful we are depends on the extent of our knowledge of the authority given us as children of God.

If you will rise up and exercise your God-given power and authority as a believer, if you will resist the devil in the name of Jesus, he will finally give up and go look for an easier target. He will leave you alone and try to find someone else who doesn't know how to resist him in the name of Jesus and the Word of God.

The Abundant Life

I am the good shepherd: the good shepherd giveth his life for the sheep.

John 10:11

Immediately after Jesus said that Satan, the enemy, comes to steal, and to kill and to destroy, but that He had come to give life more abundantly, Jesus went on to say that He is the good Shepherd because He gives His life for the sheep.

The reason Jesus gave His life for you and me is so we can have abundant life, here and now, as well as in heaven.

My brother and my sister, please get this straight: there has only been one kind of life provided for us. The life of sickness, poverty, worry, stress, anxiety and confusion that so many believers live is not the kind of life that Jesus Christ died to provide. He only provided one kind of life, not two kinds. He gave up His own life that you and I might have a life of abundance: abundant health, abundant prosperity, abundant freedom, abundant joy, abundant peace, abundant faith, abundant love.

If your life is not filled with that kind of abundance, then you are not living the true Christian life. You are allowing the enemy to rob you of the life that God intends for you to have and enjoy. You need to have your life founded upon Jesus, the Rock of your salvation.

Jesus as the Rock

Therefore whosoever heareth these sayings of mine, and doeth them, I will liken him unto a wise man, which built his house upon a rock:

And the rain descended, and the floods came, and the winds blew, and beat upon that house; and it fell not: for it was founded upon a rock.

And every one that heareth these sayings of mine, and doeth them not, shall be likened unto a foolish man, which built his house upon the sand:

And the rain descended, and the floods came, and the winds blew, and beat upon that house; and it fell: and great was the fall of it.

Matthew 7:24-27

Jesus is the Rock on which we are to build our lives. That means that there is something that we are to do in order to experience the full, abundant life that He has provided for us.

An Astonishing Doctrine

And it came to pass, when Jesus had ended these sayings, the people were astonished at his doctrine:

For he taught them as one having authority, and not as the scribes.

Matthew 7:28,29

When I teach the Word of God, people are always astonished at my doctrine — always!

Some time ago I was in a store and saw a lady standing there who had her hand to her head and was obviously suffering. Although I didn't know her, I walked over and said to her, "Do you have a headache, ma'am?"

"Oh, yes," she said, "I sure do. I have migraine headaches all the time. This one has been on me for two or three days. Sometimes they stay on me for a week, and it hurts so bad I can hardly stand it."

I looked her straight in the eye and said, "I don't put up with headaches!"

"Oh, you don't?"

"No, I don't!"

I said it loud and clear because the devil listens to nothing but the voice of authority.

About that time the woman's husband came over and saw me talking to his wife.

"Is this your husband?" I asked her.

"Yes."

Then I turned to him and said, "Sir, your wife is suffering terribly."

"Yes, I know," he said. "She has migraine headaches all the time."

"Well, I don't put up with headaches," I told him.

"You don't?"

"No, I don't! Why do you put up with them?"

The man looked at me like he didn't know what I was talking about.

At that moment, I decided to do the store manager a favor and move our discussion outdoors, so I said to the couple, "If you'll just step outside, I'll make that dumb thing leave."

"Oh, but I've had it for years..." the woman protested.

"If I pray for you, you'll never have another one," I told her.

Then I turned to her husband again and asked him, "Do you want me to pray for your wife?"

"Sure," he said.

Once we were outside, I took the woman's head in my hands and said in a loud voice, "In Jesus' name, I bind you, Satan! I command you, turn this woman's head loose! I order you to come out of her, in Jesus' name! You must obey me! Go from her! I'm not giving you any choice, go!"

You can't give the devil a choice; if you do, things will stay just as they are. As long as you give Satan a choice in the matter, your sickness or disease or infirmity will stay on you until you die.

So I just kept on taking authority over the devil, commanding him to leave the woman alone.

"How many times did you do that?"

Probably twenty or twenty-five times. And the more I did it, the stronger I got. If you ever start weakening, the devil will not obey you. Satan doesn't obey weak people. Never. The devil only responds to authority and power, that's all he listens to.

Suddenly the power of God was manifested, and the woman broke down in tears. She began to weep and weep. The glory of the Lord came upon her, and the Holy Ghost began to bubble up out of me. I started to weep too — and to get blessed.

"Why did *you* get blessed?"

Because I had broken the power of the devil. If you will bless someone else, God will bless you.

The woman wept and wept. As she was crying, I walked around glorifying God: "Thank You, Lord, because she is healed and will never have another headache. Blessed be the name of the Lord!"

By the time the woman had come to herself, after weeping with joy for five or ten minutes, I said to her, "You don't have a headache, do you?"

"Oh, no, it's gone," she said.

"Now you'll never have another headache," I told her, "if you'll just take authority over that thing in the name of Jesus."

I looked at her husband and said to him, "Sir, you are the head of your house. The next time the devil comes and tries to attack your wife with a headache, you make that dumb thing leave her!"

"Okay," he said, "but I'm not sure if I know how to do that or not."

"Yes, you do," I said. "You stood there and watched me."

"Oh, is that the way you do it?"

"That's the way you do it. There are no two ways, just one: take authority over the devil and make him obey you, in Jesus' name."

"Well, okay," he said. "All right."

"Don't let your wife have any more headaches," I warned him.

Make the Devil Obey You!

You can make the devil obey you if you speak to him with the voice of authority, in the name of Jesus.

Any person who is dying of cancer can get out his Bible, claim God's promise of healing and rebuke the destroyer. He can speak to that cancer and bind it in the name of Jesus, commanding it to go from him — and it will obey him.

But if he just sits around and waits for God to heal him, he may wait too late.

Whatever your situation, whatever your need, you must learn to put action to your faith. The Bible plainly says that without action, faith is dead. (James 2:20.) In Matthew 7:24 Jesus said that "whosoever" *hears* His sayings and *does* them is like a man who built his house on a rock.

When Jesus says, "Whosoever," He means you and me. "Whosoever" puts his faith and trust in Jesus Christ, the Rock, is a wise man. Now as wise men and women, let's look together at the last words recorded in the Gospel of Mark that Jesus spoke just before He ascended into heaven.

The Laying on of Hands for Healing

And he said unto them, Go ye into all the world, and preach the gospel to every creature.

He that believeth and is baptized shall be saved; but he that believeth not shall be damned.

And these signs shall follow them that believe; In my name shall they cast out devils; they shall speak with new tongues;

They shall take up serpents; and if they drink any deadly thing, it shall not hurt them; *they shall lay hands on the sick, and they shall recover.*

Mark 16:15-18

Notice the last eleven words spoken in this passage by Jesus just before **he was received up into heaven** (v. 19): **...they shall lay hands on the sick, and they shall recover.**

These words are so important that I wrote a book on them titled *God's Power Through the Laying on of Hands** in which I list every Scripture in the New Testament concerning the laying on of hands. Kenneth Hagin likes this book so much that he orders it by the case.

I learned about the laying on of hands from Reverend Littlefield, the Full-Gospel Pentecostal minister I have mentioned several times. Since I knew nothing about God

*See the list at the back of this book.

and His ways, I would go to Reverend Littlefield's church to learn. After a while he would say to me, "Come up here, Brother Norvel, and help us pray for the people." I would think, "Oh, brother," but I would go up to the front of the church to help with prayer.

One night I was standing at the altar when suddenly I felt power come into my hands. I walked over and said, "Reverend Littlefield, what is this going through my hands? It feels like the bones are about to jump out of my fingers. There's something alive there, I can feel it."

"That's the healing power of Jesus," he explained. Then he said to me, "Come over here, Brother Norvel, and lay your hands on this woman. She's been sick a long time."

I went over and laid my hands on the woman, and immediately she fell over.

"Oh, God," I said, "did I kill her?" That's how ignorant I was. I knew nothing about being slain in the Spirit. The reason I knew nothing about such a manifestation of the power and presence of the Spirit is because that kind of thing never happened in the church I had attended all my life.

Some time later Reverend Littlefield called and asked me to meet him at church to go pray for a woman who was living at the Methodist home. When we arrived at the home, we were joined by the woman's pastor and song leader. At her bedside, Reverend Littlefield said to the other men, "You kneel down at the end of the bed — I'm going to kneel here at the side." Then he turned to me and said, "Brother Norvel, the Lord has given me instructions for you to stand at the head of the bed and reach over and lay your hands on this lady."

So I reached out and laid my hand on her in Jesus' name. As I did so, she started to quiver, and my hand and arm began to turn warm. The bed started shaking, and I noticed that the woman was crying.

"What's happening to me?" she asked. "Something's going through me and driving out all my bad feelings. What is this?"

"That's the Lord Jesus Christ healing you," I told her.

Since then I have learned that one of the main ways that the Lord visits the sick is through the laying on of hands.

The Gift of Healing

So after that experience, I began to pray for people and lay hands on them. But I really didn't know for sure that God had given me the gift of healing until one time when I was speaking at a Christian banquet in a Holiday Inn ballroom in Pennsylvania.

While I was speaking, all of a sudden a deaf man approached me for healing. The Lord said to me, "Cast that deaf spirit out of him," so I said, "You foul deaf spirit, come out of him in the name of Jesus!"

The man fell flat on the floor just as if he had been shot. As he did so, both ears popped open.

Seeing that, the people started jumping to their feet and running down to me saying, "Pray for me! Pray for me! Pray for me!"

I reached out toward them to pray for them, and they all started falling flat on the floor everywhere, all over that packed ballroom.

I went back through the hall holding out my hands and praying for them, and they would fall over left and right. After about five minutes it looked as if someone had gone through that room with a machine gun and mowed them down.

One elderly gray-haired man about seventy-five or eighty years old came up to me and said, "Young man, I'm an old-line Pentecostal missionary, and I haven't seen power like this in fifty-five years."

I could have told him, "I've never seen it in my whole life!"

That night, my brother or sister, God gave me the power to lay hands on the sick for their healing. And that gift was given to me to abide forever. All I had to do was reach out very gently and say, "In Jesus' name, receive your healing."

Obedience Is a Sign of Wisdom

In 1976 one of the greatest miracles that has ever taken place in this country came about by the gentle touch of the laying on of hands.

One Sunday morning I was speaking to about a thousand people at a Bible school in Pensacola, Florida. I was speaking from the sixteenth chapter of Matthew when I noticed a scrawny, twisted, crippled lady sitting in a wheelchair down front.

Suddenly the Lord said to me, "I want you to lay hands on her."

I didn't even know that God did things like that. But I knew enough to be obedient. I stopped and said to the congregation, "Excuse me, the Lord wants me to pray for this lady."

I went down and gently laid my right hand on her forehead. She told us later that the moment the tips of my fingers touched her, she went unconscious. But those of us in the room saw her whole body suddenly shoot up out of that wheelchair. In the middle of the air all her crooked limbs and feet were straightened out. Although she had been 75 percent blind, her eyesight became completely normal.

This lady's name was Mae Stafford. She had suffered from cerebral palsy for more than ten years. She had sat in a wheelchair, twisted and bent, and so blind that she could hardly see. But the moment I reached out and gently touched her in Jesus' name, God picked her up out of that wheelchair and made her totally normal. Her hands and feet and sight were miraculously restored.

She was so pleased and overjoyed that she loved to show off to people how Jesus had healed her. Now she goes around the country laying hands on others, and the Lord heals them.

In Matthew 7:24 Jesus said, **Whosoever heareth these sayings of mine, and doeth them, I will liken him unto a wise man.** If you and I are wise, then we will do as Jesus said His disciples would do: we will lay hands on the sick, and they will recover.

As we continue to worship the Lord, have faith in Him, do the work that He has called us to do and increase in knowledge of Him and obedience to Him, He will continue to perform miracles in our lives and ministries.

Norvel Hayes shares God's Word boldly and simply, with an enthusiasm that captures the heart of the hearer. He has learned through personal experience that God's Word can be effective in every area of life and that it will work for anyone who will believe it and apply it.

Norvel owns several businesses which function successfully despite the fact that he spends more than half his time away from the office, ministering the Gospel throughout the country. His obedience to God and his willingness to share his faith have taken him to a variety of places. He ministers in churches, seminars, conventions, colleges, prisons — anywhere the Spirit of God leads.

For a complete list of tapes and books
by Norvel Hayes, write:

Norvel Hayes
P. O. Box 1379
Cleveland, TN 37311

Please include your prayer requests
and comments when you write.

Books by Norvel Hayes

Divine Healing — God's Recipe for Life and Health

Worship

Confession Brings Possession

Let Not Your Heart Be Troubled

Endued With Power

How To Live and Not Die

The Winds of God Bring Revival

God's Power Through the Laying On of Hands

The Blessing of Obedience

Visions — The Window to the Supernatural

Stand in the Gap for Your Children

How To Get Your Prayers Answered

Number One Way To Fight the Devil

Why You Should Speak in Tongues

Misguided Faith

What To Do for Healing

Financial Dominion — How To Take Charge of Your Finances

Rescuing Souls From Hell — Handbook for Effective Soulwinning

How To Cast Out Devils

Radical Christianity

Secrets To Keeping Your Faith Strong

Putting Your Angels To Work

Know Your Enemy

Available from your local bookstore.

For additional copies in Canada,
contact:

Word Alive
P. O. Box 670
Niverville, Manitoba
CANADA R0A 1E0

The Harrison House Vision

Proclaiming the truth and the power
Of the Gospel of Jesus Christ
With excellence;

Challenging Christians to
Live victoriously,
Grow spiritually,
Know God intimately.